HOME
BY
DESIGN

SARAH SUSANKA
HOME BY DESIGN

Transforming
Your House into Home

The Taunton Press

The Taunton Press, Inc.
63 South Main Street, PO Box 5506
Newtown, CT 06470-5506
e-mail: tp@taunton.com

Distributed by Publishers Group West

EDITOR: Peter Chapman
INTERIOR DESIGN: David Bullen
LAYOUT: Carol Petro
ILLUSTRATOR: Vincent Babak
PHOTOGRAPHER: Grey Crawford, except where noted

LIBRARY OF CONGRESS CATALOGING-IN-PUBLICATION DATA
Susanka, Sarah.
  Home by design : transforming your house into home / Sarah Susanka.
    p. cm.
Includes index.
  ISBN 1-56158-618-8
  1. Architecture, Domestic--United States. 2. Architecture--United States--20th century. 3. Architcture--United States--21st century. 4. Architecture, Domestic--Designs and plans. I. Title.
NA7208.S884 2004
728'.37'0973--dc22
                        2003026583

This book is dedicated to Christopher Alexander, architect and author of A Pattern Language, *who through his research and writings helped shape the dreams and aspirations of a new generation of architects, builders, and the people they serve.*

IT SEEMS LIKE ONLY A FEW SHORT MONTHS AGO that the book you now hold in your hands was a solid wall of photographs and Post-It notes covering the interior of my writing studio in North Carolina. Of all the four books I've written, this one has been the most challenging to put together, and I'm truly grateful for the wonderful organizational skills of my assistant and dear friend Marie St. Hilaire, who helped keep everything straight. The photographs that illustrate this book were taken from 30 different houses across the country (culled from an original submission of over 200 houses), each one chosen to illustrate a specific design principle. The challenge was then to assemble the photographs and the words, like a giant jigsaw puzzle, into a cohesive whole.

The photographs themselves were taken by California photographer Grey Crawford, who also worked on my second book, *Creating the Not So Big House.* Grey has an eye for the perfect shot and an uncanny ability to capture on film the design principles I'm explaining in words. Thanks again, Grey. I'd also like to thank all the architects who are featured in this book and, of course, the owners who allowed us to photograph their "homes by design."

My old friend Peter Chapman, a senior editor at The Taunton Press, has worked with me on each of my four books, and by this point we each know pretty well how the other one thinks. We make a great team. Also at Taunton, my thanks go out to art director Paula Schlosser, photo editor Wendi Mijal, and design manager Carol Singer, who helped compose all the materials to make the finished book a work of beauty and clarity. Thanks also to layout artist Carol Petro.

There are many, many other players at The Taunton Press as well, all of whom help to make the experience of writing a book not only successful but also enjoyable. Although I don't have room here to describe the roles that each of them plays, a huge thank you to Maria Taylor, Allison Hollett, Carolyn Mandarano, Lynne Phillips, Robyn Doyon Aitken, and Amy Reilly.

And, finally, my gratitude goes to Jim Childs, the book publisher at Taunton, who has become a good friend as well as a wonderful advocate and promoter of my work. As an author, I couldn't wish for a more insightful or enthusiastic partner in bringing my ideas to market. You may also be glad to know that between the two of us, we have my life planned out in book-writing ventures for quite a few years into the future. So I hope you'll stay tuned. There's more to come.

CONTENTS

HOME BY DESIGN IS THE BOOK I'VE ALWAYS WANTED TO WRITE. About 10 years ago, I started work on a book about principles of design that I hoped would enable homeowners, builders, interior designers, and architects to start talking with one another about what makes a house a "home." But along the way, I became fascinated with the state of residential architecture in this country, and out of this fascination was born my first book, *The Not So Big House*.

The Not So Big House offered a different vision of home, one that values quality over quantity, and the book produced a groundswell of enthusiastic believers. *Not So Big* was even dubbed a movement. *Creating the Not So Big House* and *Not So Big Solutions for Your Home* followed, fleshing out the message and helping explain how to tailor a house to fit the lives lived within its walls.

And now, finally, it's time for the book whose principles are embedded in each of the previous three. It's time for the book I dreamed of all those years ago—*Home by Design*. Organized into three sections, Space, Light, and Order, the chapters of the book take on one design principle at a time, explaining what it is, how and why it works, and how it can be incorporated into your home. So, for example, in the chapter on Alignments, the applications are Perfect Symmetry; Partial Symmetry; Asymmetry; View along a Main Axis; If in Doubt, Line It Up; and Half a Bubble Off. All of these terms are part of the architect's toolbox, but no one has ever illustrated them, explained them in jargon-free language, and made them accessible to a wide audience.

Good architectural design is every bit as important as good nutrition. Both are good medicine for our physical and spiritual well-being, and a lack of either one can cause a myriad of unnecessary maladies. You'll find that there is a rhyme and a reason to what you feel about the place you call home, and this book will help you understand how to craft your own surroundings into a better place to live.

From House to Home

I FIRST STARTED THINKING ABOUT BUYING A HOUSE in early spring of 1986. I didn't have a lot of money, so I knew I'd be looking for an existing home. I made a list of all the rooms I wanted, estimated how much space I'd need, and chose the community I wanted to live in—a lovely older neighborhood of small but well cared for homes along streets lined with stately elm trees.

Then one Saturday morning, as I was walking through the area, I found it. It was a house I'd passed before, but now there was a "For Sale by Owner" sign on the front lawn. The house wasn't much to look at—a square, turn-of-the-century, stucco box with a steep roof and nondescript green trim. But there was something about it that appealed to me, and as I walked up the path to the front door, with its full pane of intricate Victorian art glass, I started to get a good feeling about the house.

The homeowner answered the door, and almost instantly, before I'd even set foot inside, I knew that this was *it*—this was the house for me. As I stood there on the threshold, all my thoughts about rooms and square footage fell by the wayside as I succumbed to the indefinable something that said "home" to me. From the doorstep, I could look through two arched openings, both surrounded by wide oak trim, past a light-filled living room to a dining room at the opposite corner of the house. Although I couldn't see the entire room from where I stood, the dining room windows seemed to beckon to me, to encourage me to come on in and explore.

At the homeowner's invitation I went inside, and before the day was over I'd set the wheels in motion to become the new owner.

After this first home-buying experience, I started thinking about

The impression created by the front door deeply influences how we experience the rest of the house. Here, there's a strong sense of symmetry and order.

footage, the dimensions of a room, and the adjacencies of one room to another as though these alone can secure comfort, when in fact it is the interrelationships between spaces, walls and ceilings, and windows that shape our experience. These basic ingredients are the tools by which we give form to our interior environment, and though they seem simple enough, there's much more that can be done with them than most people realize. The problem is that most would-be homeowners assume that they need to select a style of architecture, such as Colonial, Georgian, or Prairie, to establish a particular character for their house. But although a style can define the exterior character, very few houses do much to distinguish themselves stylistically on the interior. Yet the interior is where we live, and where we really care about creating the feeling of home.

So if the style of a house doesn't guarantee a particular character and quality of interior space, what does? In fact, there's something even more fundamental than style, but we don't really have a name for it. If you peel away the surface stylistic embellishments, you'll find some basic principles that govern the ordering of space and light to create the experiences of home that we crave. A house that's been designed using these principles is a Home by Design. The alternative, which happens when these principles are not understood, is a house that provides adequate shelter and plenty of

what this "it" feeling was all about. Was there a way to quantify it, or to replicate it? Were there ways to describe it so that you could discuss it and tell others about it? What I discovered is that although almost everyone I spoke with about "it" knew what I was talking about, not one of them had the words to explain what "it" is.

The Elusive Quality of Home

So began a 20-year-long adventure into defining the elusive quality of "home." Over time, I came to understand that although many people have a highly developed sense of space, because we don't have a common language to describe our spatial experiences, we've resorted to talking in terms of size and volume rather than in terms of the qualities of the space. We speak of square

Revealing a partial view of a space and placing a window at the end of a visual axis are two tools that architects use to draw people from place to place in a home.

Contrast can make a room more dynamic and engaging. Here, the green door stands out against the white walls, focusing our attention.

square footage but that lacks the qualities of home.

Even architects to this point have had no consistent terminology for these principles, so these principles have rarely been committed to print in language that nonarchitects can understand. The names given to them, as well as to their applications in the home, will provide a common vocabulary for everyone involved in the making of houses, so that homeowners can explain what they are looking for and in turn be understood by those they hire to help them. This book, then, is a guide to what underlies

style, and to what transforms an ordinary house into home.

The Architect's Toolbox

It might look effortless on television or in a magazine, but when it comes to making your own home a place that delights you, you'll quickly discover there are lots of things you need to know that require skill and training. Although architects and interior designers have the knowledge to help you, what's missing is a way to describe the spatial experience that is understandable to anyone with a desire for a

Space

Light

Order

comfortable and beautiful home. What's needed is a look inside the architect's "toolbox"—the principles architects use to sculpt space and light, to imbue their creations with a sense of order, and in so doing, turn basic square footage and volume into exceptional living space. These principles fall into three basic categories.

SPACE

First of all, there are principles having to do with space—with how volume can be shaped, molded, and divided to give you a particular kind of spatial experience. For example, most homes have ceilings that are all one height. There might be a cathedral ceiling in the living room, but other than that, the ceilings are all a standard 8 ft. or 9 ft. high—which can be pretty monotonous. The principle called Ceiling Height Variety explains how you can vary the heights of parts of rooms, as well as the connections between spaces, to define one activity place from another, without resorting to solid walls. This results in a house that's more open from place to place but that also has a greater sense of intimacy to it. So the whole house ends up feeling more comfortable.

One of the most important things to understand here is that we experience space not so much by quantity alone, but by the interconnections between one chunk of space and another. When space is divided into discrete but visible areas, our senses tell us there's more there. It works on the same principle that parents use when asking a young child how many pieces of bread he or she wants for breakfast. When you cut one slice into four pieces, the child assumes she's getting more than if you were to leave the bread uncut. The eye recognizes multiple segments whether it's slices of bread or chunks of space and reads more.

LIGHT

The second category in the architect's toolbox is light. In many ways we take light for granted. We put windows and skylights into the wall and ceiling surfaces to bring daylight into the interior of a house. And we scatter light fixtures around to provide artificial light for the places and times of day when and where daylight isn't available. But if you've ever been to a truly beautifully designed building, you may have noticed that the lighting gives the structure an almost transcendent quality. It not only enlivens the

space but also somehow draws attention to the surfaces of the building in a way that makes you want to explore it more.

Light is the great animator of space, and when placed with an artist's eye, it can make even a simple square room into a place you'll enjoy being in. It doesn't require a big budget to transform a very plain structure into a visual feast, just by understanding where to locate windows and light fixtures for maximum effect. For example, if you place a window or skylight directly adjacent to a perpendicular wall, the entire space is flooded with daylight, giving it a brighter, cheerier feel. This is the principle called Reflecting Surfaces, and it's a valuable tool in enlivening even the simplest of structures.

ORDER

The third, and final, category is what architects refer to as order. This simply means the way in which the elements in a design are arranged to give it an identity all its own. The room shown below, for example, illustrates a couple of principles relating to order. In terms of Alignments, the room is symmetrically organized around its centerline. There is also a distinct Rhythm to the space, created by the beams in the ceiling. And finally the room has a signature pattern—a set of small squares that form part of the lattice on either side of the window bay—that appears not only here but also in various places throughout the house. So it's a house that has a Theme and Variations. Most houses are lacking features like these that tell you, as you move from room to room, that they are all parts of a singular whole. But a house that's a Home by Design has some underlying organizational features that help identify it as all one thing, no matter where you are in the house.

Space, light, order. This space is separated into two distinct activity places by the raised platform at the window bay and the patterned screens—implied walls—to either side. The brightness of the windows draws us toward the bay, and the repetition of square geometric patterns gives the entire space its own distinct order and identity.

The doorway is located on the right side of the house, underneath a covered stoop that welcomes visitors even before they are met at the door.

Once inside the vestibule, the materials change, but there are still echoes of the exterior—like the light fixture and the coloring of the lower part of the wall. It is an in-between zone of the house, not quite inside and not quite out.

runs the entire width of the house, but it is far more interesting than a standard hallway would be. What makes this view particularly intriguing, and what draws you into the space, is the partially hidden view of the dining room, which makes you want to see more. This is just one of the devices you can use to make a house more engaging. Although we usually design our homes to take advantage of the exterior views through the windows, we rarely design the views from one interior space to another.

Look at the view at the end of the entry hallway, for example (see the photo on pp. 10–11). Your eyes are attracted by the window at the far end. It is an excellent example of a principle that architects use all the time to draw you from place to place without your knowing it. It's what I call Light to Walk Toward, which you'll learn about in more detail in Chapter 14.

A few steps inside and your attention is captured by another window to the right that's aligned with the short lowered hallway into the main living area. A more private and intimate area of the house is revealed, and the windows of the informal eating area invite you in. You move into the main living area, which is really a Sequence of Places, rather than a set of discrete rooms. What makes this living area different from the standard great room is the use of varying ceiling heights to identify one place from the next, without using walls (which you'll learn about in Chapter 4). None of the spaces is particularly tall or grand, yet each is clearly a separate activity place, and all of them work well together.

Throughout the house, varying ceiling heights are used to define different activity places. A wide soffit over the kitchen peninsula and a lowered ceiling in the eating alcove both lend a sense of shelter to the seating below.

In fact, Ceiling Height Variety is used throughout the house to sculpt the various rooms to serve their functions better. In the mudroom, connecting the house with the garage, the coat-hanging and mail-sorting places have been differentiated from the hallway by a dropped ceiling that gives each function a discrete identity, as well as a sense of shelter. Without the change in ceiling height, it turns into a standard, rather nondescript back entrance, with little or no order to it. It's the way the room has been divided into several pieces, just like the example of the slice of bread, that makes it more appealing.

PICTURE THIS

Without the dropped ceiling over the coat rack and mail-sorting place, the mudroom loses a lot of its character. (You'll find many examples of modified photos like this throughout the book.)

Contrast and Illusion Architects are magicians of space and light, where magic is simply something that isn't readily understood by just looking at it. They use the art of illusion to make less seem like more, and they use contrast, like the difference between a bright window and a darker surrounding wall, to make our senses take note.

In the photo shown here, take a look at the trim line that surrounds the dining room, just above window height. This line is used consistently throughout the home, with a different color of paint applied above and below the line. The contrast between the colors, combined with the separation of the wall surface into two parts, tells our senses, inaccurately as it turns out, that the ceiling is higher than it actually is. This allows the rooms to retain their more appropriately human-scaled dimensions, while still giving them a spacious feel.

A Sense of Order

When I design a new house like this, I'll work on the designs for both the outside and the inside simultaneously, to give the whole a sense of order and integrity. On the outside, I try to give the house a shape that fits into the neighborhood, so in this case I used a simple, square form that resembles the surrounding houses. I think about the composition of roof forms, so that the relative proportions of windows to wall surfaces, overhangs, and roof slope all combine to look pleasing to the eye.

The same kind of consideration is given to the inside as well. To make the final configuration of spaces flow naturally and gracefully, an architect will typically do a number of iterations of the layout, trying to find a solution in which all the parts fall effortlessly together. The upstairs landing for this house presented some interesting challenges on this front. There were five doors, all needing to open into their respective rooms—three bedrooms,

a bathroom, and a laundry. After studying several versions of the plan, I arrived at a landing shape that's basically an elongated octagon. The familiar geometrical form lends an order to the space, which might otherwise seem overwhelmed with doors. The octagon is an organizing feature that gives you a way of relating to the multiplicity of entries in a different way.

These issues of composition, proportion, and organization on both the interior and exterior are principles of Order. Just as you might organize the piles of paper on your desk to make it easier to find what you'll need later, so these ordering principles allow us to grasp what we are looking at and experiencing, with a minimum of confusion.

A long diagonal view from the landing into the master bedroom makes the second floor seem larger than it really is. The brightness of the window-seat wall instinctively draws us into the room.

Putting It All Together

You can see how all three of these primary ingredients of design—space, light, and order—come together in this home's master bedroom. The ceiling has been crafted to emphasize the center of the room, the tallest area, but in so doing it gives a sense of shelter to the areas beneath the lowered ceilings—the bed, the window seat, and the entrance to the room. Daylight reflects off the sidewall of the window seat, providing a bright spot that draws you into the space, while the painted wall behind the bed lends the room a distinct Point of Focus. Like the landing, the entire composition is given an overarching order by the shape of the taller ceiling, which has a much simpler form than

SECOND FLOOR

Bedroom

Landing

Laundry

Master bedroom

Bedroom

At the upstairs landing, an octagonal ceiling helps give some order to a space ringed by five doors.

that of the perimeter walls. What could have been just an ordinary, and rather amorphous bedroom, with an 8-ft. ceiling, has been turned into a place of elegant comfort and quiet remove.

One of the key themes woven throughout this book is the importance of using our natural, physiological instincts regarding space and light to vitalize a design, and to make it feel like "home." Throughout this design, I used our inclination to move toward light to literally steer people through the house. I used ceiling height variations to give shelter and intimacy to some activity places and to give added importance to others. And I used simple geometrical forms and patterns to make the house more intelligible, and therefore more approachable and welcoming. In fact, if I think back to the story of the purchase of my first home, I now understand that it was the allure of the dining room windows at the far corner of the house from the front door, combined with the differentiation of living spaces defined by a series of simple arched openings, that gave the house such a strong quality of home.

So that feeling of "this is *it*" turns out to be something definable after all. Although it can't be summed up in just a word or two, its attributes can be described, and it can be designed into a house, whether new or remodeled, to give it that ineffable quality that makes us want to settle in and stay

A continuous trim band runs around all the rooms, the lowered ceilings falling at the height of its bottom edge.

Obscuring art glass in the windows on the sides of the house lets in daylight but blocks unwanted views of the neighboring houses, which are only a few feet away.

Great Buildings

Many of the design principles related to houses can also be applied to public buildings, such as this dramatic library at Exeter University, designed by architect Louis Kahn.

This view across the central atrium illustrates a number of key principles. The architect carefully crafted the interior views, so that you are not only oriented within the building but also have something beautiful to look at no matter where you are in the library. This is an application of the principle called Interior Views, which you'll read about in Chapter 5. The huge circles use an Archetypal Form, which is discussed in Chapter 23, Theme and Variations. In combination with the wood guardrails and library shelves behind, the composition is also an excellent illustration of Layering, which you'll read about in Chapter 6.

After reading the chapters that follow, you'll be able to recognize many of these principles in the public architecture that surrounds you, not just in your own home.

a while. Just like love, the chemistry between house and homeowner must be compelling, or all the preplanning to get the right number, size, and location of rooms will be worthless. Specifics alone are not enough. Though they can secure basic shelter and a degree of functionality, they are not enough to supply the ingredients that will provide delight on a daily basis.

This is the part of the house selection process that's been missing until now. With no words to describe the qualities of home that we so long for, we settle for much less than we know is possible and then are disappointed when it doesn't satisfy our desire for something more. This book will help give you the words you need to identify what it is that lends vitality to a house and transforms it into a place you'll really love for the long term.

It's really not that mysterious, but simply requires that you be able to look beneath the surface style to the principles of space, light, and order that animate it. When you really understand the concepts that follow, you'll know what it takes to turn your house into home, and you'll know that home isn't something accidental or ephemeral. "It" comes about "by design."

PART ONE

Space

preceded by the phrases "too little" or "lots of." In other words,
we tend to conceive of space only in terms of quantities. But the way
that architects use space is quite different. To us, it is our primary
tool in the shaping of experience. We sculpt space in much the
same way that a potter shapes clay to form a container, such as a
vase or a pitcher. But where the focus of the potter's work is
primarily the "exterior" of the object, for architects it is equally on
the interior, where people live, work, and play. We quite literally
shape the interior spaces to make better, more comfortable, and
more engaging "containers" for the activities that take place within.

There's so much more that's possible when you understand the
malleability of this medium we call space. It's capable of giving us
an extraordinary variety of experiences that can delight us spatially
and accommodate our lives and our needs in ways we'd never
dreamed of.

ONE

The Process of Entering

Designing an entryway includes not only the doorway but also the series of places you pass through as you move from the street or driveway to the front stoop, and on into the house.

THERE'S NOTHING MORE CRITICAL to the experience of a house than the impression it sets for both visitor and homeowner. Even from the street or driveway, a house can be designed to give signals that your presence is desired. A house with even a small front porch or covered stoop, for example, tells visitors that there is a place for them to stand, a place where the house receives them, even before anyone comes to answer the door. If it's raining, you won't get wet, and if it takes a minute or two for the homeowner to answer, you don't feel that you are trespassing. It's as though the house had reached out to you in welcome and is giving you permission to be there until the door is opened.

We've all experienced houses that are the antithesis of this—the house with no cover over the entry, no landing at the top of the steps from the pathway to the door, and no windows in or around the door to let you know that someone has heard your arrival. Standing in the rain, with one foot on the top step, one on the step below, wondering if anyone inside knows that you are there, is hardly the kind of welcome that most of us would wish for our guests. And it hardly sets the stage for a positive experience of the rest of the house.

A well-designed entry needs to include everything from the view from the street to the experience of waiting at the door to the space you're received into once the door has been opened and you've been welcomed in. The whole sequence needs to be designed to allow you to change from the public person that you are when outside in the world to the much more private person that you are once inside.

Path and Place

The edge of the property marks the boundary between the public world of streets and cars and the more private world of the house and its occupants. The Process of Entering starts at the street or driveway and leads the visitor from that point, across the property line, and up to the front door. So the path between the two, as well as the place that you arrive at the front door, sets the stage for what you'll find once inside. By using materials and shapes that reinforce the character of the home, the experience of path and place becomes part of a singular, integrated whole.

The house shown here and on p. 20 is filled with curves and rounded forms, and the path and waiting place reflect this. The brick landing at the door is ample, and the low walls to either side emphasize the sense of arrival. The path can also have intermediate places along the way, like the small bench tucked into the border of flowers.

Receiving Place

Once the door has been opened and the guest or homeowner steps inside, there needs to be a place to stand for a moment to get oriented to the house and to make the transition from the way we are when in the more public realm to the way we are in a more private setting. Typically, we think of this as the foyer and give it no further thought, but it's really more than that. It's a place of personal metamorphosis that also offers a preview of what the rest of the house is like. If we are gracefully received by this area, we have positive expectations about the rest of the home.

It's important to give careful attention to how you shape this space. A very tall space, such as a two-story entryway, can make you feel overwhelmed and insignificant, whereas a tiny space with barely room to stand can make you feel cramped and awkward. Ideally, this area should be large enough for two or three people to stand and talk comfortably and should offer interesting glimpses of other areas of the house.

Gateways

If you want to emphasize the edge of the property, or the boundary of the home's territory, you can use a gateway, which essentially serves as an entry into the landscape surrounding the house. It can be as simple as two posts, one either side of the path that leads to the house, or it can be a more elaborate affair like the one shown here. The latticework above the entry creates an implied ceiling that marks the transition between inside and outside.

In the same way you can use a gateway outside the house to indicate that you are moving into the territory of the home, you can do much the same inside the house with an interior gateway between two rooms or areas. This type of gateway is a bit like a wide doorway without a door in it, and it can take any number of different shapes, from an archway to a broad opening flanked by columns to an elaborate framed opening (which we'll discuss more in chapter 6, Layering). Like a gate, it draws attention to the passage between one area and another.

Entry Courtyard

In addition to a gateway, you can also surround a segment of the territory adjacent to the home's entry with a fence or wall to create a courtyard. This outdoor receiving room provides a pronounced separation between inner and outer worlds and gives the interior of the home a more intimate, more sheltered quality as a result.

When the wall enclosure provides significant visual privacy from the street, the courtyard can also be used for outdoor family activities that would more typically occur in the backyard. This can be a valuable tool where space is tight, and there's a desire for some extra private outdoor space. Even when space is plentiful, you'll often see this technique used in hot climates, where the added shade offered by the surrounding walls makes more of the outdoor space useable during daylight hours.

Covered Entry

Providing a small segment of roof or overhang above an entry door can make a huge difference to the sense of welcome that the house extends to you and your guests. Without one, there's no protection from the elements and no sense that your presence is desired. With one, a guest can wait comfortably while the door is answered. The house has extended itself out to receive the guest even before the door is opened. The cover does not need to be large. At minimum, it should extend out 2 ft. 6 in. from the surface of the door and should direct rainwater away from the path below. This can be done either with a gutter and downspout or by sloping the roof as in the photo shown below.

Front Porch

There's a resurgence of interest today in the front porch. This is due in part to its symbolic reference to simpler times, when families would sit in the evenings and visit with one another and with their neighbors. But there's another reason for our interest as well, which is less well understood but perhaps more significant. The front porch creates an outdoor room that, like the entry courtyard, provides a bit of separation between street and house, increasing the sense of intimacy of the interior of the home.

When we describe porches we often use the word "gracious." This is appropriate because the porch further extends the covered entry's welcoming embrace. The house receives the visitor into one of its "rooms" before you officially enter the house proper.

Welcome Home

THIS HOME—a remodeling in the Connecticut countryside, designed by architect Jennifer Huestis—has all the ingredients of a wonderful entry. As you move from the driveway to the front door, you are received onto a slightly raised **front porch**, its roof supported on either side by a couple of well-proportioned columns. Even though these columns are much wider than are actually needed for support purposes, our eyes tell us that they look just right. Touches like these give the house a strong sense of quality and craftsmanship. Other small details add Old World charm, like the small stones used in the steps' risers and the traditional light fixture centered above the door.

Instead of a uniquely crafted front door, Huestis chose something more in keeping with the classically styled home: a four-panel door with flanking sidelights. The door itself is painted a contrasting color to the surrounding trim and siding so that it attracts attention and makes it

clearly the focus of the entry process. This is a simple and inexpensive approach to making a door special. Sometimes, as here, the most basic of strategies can have as powerful an impact as a more expensive approach.

One disturbing characteristic of many entryways is that guests, standing and waiting for the door to be answered, cannot tell whether the doorbell has actually sounded. They've pushed the button, but can't hear the ring from outside the

A receiving place is a critical part of the entry sequence. This one offers views through interior gateways to each of the surrounding rooms and spaces, which helps prepare the visitor for what's to come.

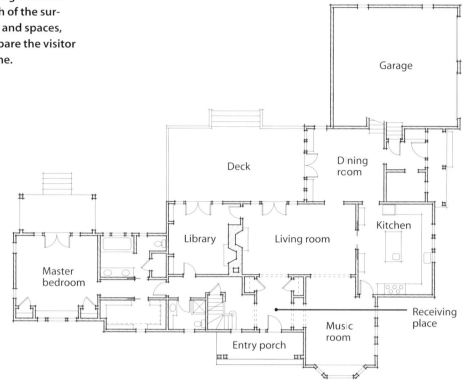

Garage

Deck

Dining room

Library

Living room

Kitchen

Master bedroom

Receiving place

Entry porch

Music room

house. In this house, guests can hear the doorbell ringing inside, and can see through the sidelights if anyone is coming to the door. Although some homeowners are concerned about privacy and about someone on the porch being able to see into the house, it's important to have at least a little glass in the door itself, or flanking it. If the privacy concern is a big issue, you can always use obscuring glass. Guests will still be able to discern movement and know when someone is coming to answer the door.

There's another major benefit to having windows in and around the doorway. A light-filled foyer is far more welcoming than one that is dark and dreary. As you step inside this home, you are greeted by a vestibule of sorts, **a receiving place,** that is flooded with light from the sidelights and from the adjacent window. The space is not enclosed with doors, but is defined by interior

A good entry, this one flanked by double columns, creates a sense of welcome even before the door is opened.

gateways that lead to each of the adjacent spaces. Each gateway (or framed opening) has an upper transom that is very similar in design to the sidelights flanking the doorway, and each demarks the entry into the next space. If you were to take away these gateways, as shown in the photo at right below, there would be no definition to the entry vestibule and no implied containment to the activity of being received into the house.

The space itself is not large, but it allows ample room for two or three people to stand, take off coats, and be greeted and welcomed into the house by the homeowners. The coat closets, one on either side of the space, are easily accessible and accentuate the graceful symmetry of this area. It's interesting to note that although this room is symmetrical, very little else in the house is so. The views to the stairway on one side of the vestibule and to the music room on the other are anything but symmetrical, yet the framed openings that lead to these areas are perfectly aligned with one another. Likewise, the **framed opening** directly across from the front door and the French doors on the opposite side of the living room are all in

alignment. Often in good design you'll find that symmetry is used sparingly but effectively, as here. It serves to draw attention to a particular spot, telling you that it is a focal point in the house, a place of confluence and harmony.

We often talk about the importance of first impressions, and this is a key function of a house's receiving place. It sets the stage for the experience of the rest of the interior. In this home, as you look toward the stairway from the vestibule, you see an interior view that is a beautiful composition of elements. The light from the adjacent window bathes the area in daylight and emphasizes the contrast in color among the natural wood stair treads, the white risers, and the lyrical line of the darker stained handrail.

An entryway can be greatly enhanced by an interior view such as this. It's a peaceful place to rest the eye, and it gives a clear impression of the simple beauty of form and color that is to come throughout the rest of the house. There are also two longer views available from this vestibule, one to the music room and the other into the main living area. Both of these are composed with the

A staircase can provide some wonderful built-in sculpture for an entryway, but it doesn't always have to be front and center. Here the stairway is located to the left of the doorway, through a framed opening.

Special Front Door

Although the Process of Entering is created by much more than just the door itself, there is certainly value in making the door leaf a special object or a more personal expression. This can be done in a number of ways. You can take a standard door and add some art glass as shown here. You can select a specially crafted front door from a door manufacturer. Or you can have a door specially built by a local craftsperson. Although this is typically the most expensive option, it provides a very personal touch to the house, that is worth the extra money.

When working with a local craftsperson, I like to make the front door a little wider than standard—3 ft. 4 in. is my preference, instead of the typical 3ft. 0 in.—to emphasize the sense of arrival. If you plan to have glass in the door but are concerned about visual privacy, you may want to use art glass that obscures the view into the house but still allows light to enter.

same kind of care, giving the visitor an impression of the spaces and places to come without divulging everything all at once.

The whole entry process gives friends and family alike a graceful transition from outside to in and offers a way to become involved gradually, rather than instantaneously, in the activities going on within the home. This carefully crafted journey of **paths and places** makes an entry process that prepares you to like whatever comes next.

TWO

Shelter around Activity

Many activities that we engage in every day in our homes benefit greatly from having some spatial definition surrounding them or partially sheltering them from adjacent spaces.

AVE YOU EVER NOTICED that when you are looking for a comfortable place to sit, you'll often select a corner rather than the center of the room? Why is this? The corner offers a sense of protection for your back. Since our vision is limited to seeing only what's in front and to the sides of our bodies, we are hard wired to favor places that ensure that our backs are safe. Although this isn't typically something we think about consciously, our actions indicate the importance of this principle. Think about when you go to a restaurant. If the host leads you to a table in the middle of the dining area, you'll probably ask if there is a booth available or at least a table at the edge of the seating area. Corners are the prized spots. We don't even question why we have these preferences. We simply know we're more comfortable in these locations.

When it comes to home design we can use this natural human inclination to great advantage. The whole house can be made to feel more comfortable and welcoming by adding a suggestion of shelter around each activity place. A corner automatically provides this sense of protection, but there are many other ways of creating the same effect. By adding an alcove, for example, the area it contains is distinguished from the rest of the room as a distinct place that can accommodate a separate activity. Or a lowered ceiling can differentiate a peripheral activity space from the focal part of a room.

Creating a sense of shelter around each activity area can make a space seem much larger than it actually is, because our eyes and senses perceive multiple defined places and we assume there must be more floor area there as a result. This principle is one of the keys to doing more with less.

Alcoves

EATING AREA WITH ALCOVE
Less square footage but more shelter around activity and more comfort

EATING AREA WITHOUT ALCOVE
More square footage but less spatial definition and less comfort

An alcove is a pocket of space that is attached to a larger room or area and is often used to house a separate activity from the function of the main room. So, for example, a rectangular family room might gain a small alcove to accommodate a computer desk and homework station. In the photo above, the informal eating area off the kitchen is nestled in an alcove with a lowered ceiling that's sheathed in wood paneling to further differentiate it from the main room. By bringing the walls in and the ceiling down around the activity place, a sense of shelter is created. Without these sheltering surfaces, although there might be more overall floor area, the table would appear to float in the available space and would be less comfortable to sit in.

An inexpensive way to create an alcove when remodeling is to take a rectangular room and build shelves or bookcases in from the wall, as shown here, to surround a

piece of furniture or small activity place. Just the suggestion of the lowered ceiling and flanking walls made by the shelves gives this couch a greater sense of belonging, and an increased sense of shelter.

Window Seats

A window seat is a particular kind of alcove—one with a built-in bench that stretches the length of the space and has a view both to the room it is part of and to the surrounding landscape. It has a wonderful in-between quality to it, not completely inside but not quite outside either.

When the ceiling is dropped down a little, as here, to enhance the sense of shelter, the space becomes a personal sanctuary. The definition given to the space by the containing walls makes it a discrete activity place that is temporarily "owned" by the person who sits there.

Many people love the look and feel of a window seat, but they rarely understand why. It's because it offers the occupant a degree of comfort and peaceful remove that's created by the surrounding walls, ceiling, and floor that define it. This kind of sitting place implies a quality of intimacy and ease that's missing in most homes today.

Soffits

A soffit is defined as "the underside of a part or member of a building." In colloquial usage, we're most familiar with the word in reference to the underside of a roof overhang on the exterior of a building. An interior soffit has a slightly different meaning, referring to a narrow section of ceiling that's lower than the rest of the ceiling surface in the room. It's usually framed down from the primary ceiling joists or roof rafters, sculpting the space below into an identifiable area that's different in character from the rest of the room.

In the photo above, the soffit effectively creates a shelter for the vanity area. The dropped ceiling in the top right photo on the facing page is also a soffit, one that's gently curved to accentuate its nestlike character. Both these soffits provide a sense of protection for the activity taking place beneath. A continuous soffit built around the perimeter of a room accentuates the height of the middle of the space.

Ceiling Shape

Another way to create a sense of shelter around an activity area is to sculpt the ceiling shape. In the library hallway shown here, the ceiling is gently curved, as though it were reaching down toward the floor with protective arms. Looking along the hall, you can sense the cocoon-like quality of the space. A ceiling that slopes downward on two or more sides accentuates the sheltering quality of the room.

Another example of a sheltering ceiling shape is a vaulted ceiling, probably the most common ceiling other than a completely flat surface. Unfortunately, many vaulted or cathedral ceilings are too tall for the floor space they cover and are commonly painted white, which tends to emphasize their height. There are many things you can do to the ceiling to help bring it into proportion with the scale of the activity areas beneath it, such as finishing the surface a darker color. You can read more about this in Chapter 19, Visual Weight.

Rug-Defined Place

The previous examples are all structural solutions to creating a sense of shelter, but you can also accomplish the same with the floor surface. By placing a rug beneath a furniture arrangement, such as the dining table shown here, you are defining the boundaries of the activity area, which in turn makes it feel sheltered. Without the rug, this room would seem rather bare and the table and chairs would appear to float in the room. The rug grounds them to this particular spot.

When the budget is limited, this application provides an inexpensive way to give a sense of shelter to an activity area. And when a room is a bit too large for the activity it is housing, a rug can really help to give it a sense of belonging.

Shelter by the Sea

This simple L-shaped house at The Sea Ranch, in northern California, designed by the architecture firm Turnbull, Griffin, Haesloop, illustrates the principle of Shelter around Activity in several ways. Although the floor plan is quite open, the **ceiling shape** in each room is designed to focus attention on and provide a strong sense of shelter for the activities below.

The dining area sits at the heart of the living space and is positioned in such a way that it falls directly below the ridge of the gable-roofed entry alcove. On the other axis, it sits close to the center of the main ridge that runs the length of the house and is exactly centered between two decorative

Throughout this simple home, the ceiling shape is used to create a sense of shelter for the activities happening below. Here, the ceiling is vaulted, providing a protective canopy over the dining table.

trusses that define the edges of the "room." The roof rafters and trusses focus attention on the table and create a sense of shelter, even though the ceiling is quite high throughout the space. To complete the composition, another feature further accentuates the activity place—a large colorful rug that grounds the table and chairs within the area.

The kitchen also gains a sense of shelter from the roof truss that falls between it and the dining area, as well as from the refrigerator and pantry at either end of the U-shaped room. These two "objects" are enclosed in wood walls and help define the kitchen as a separate **alcove**. They symbolically and visually stake the edges of the space. Without them the kitchen would seem far less sheltered. If the ceiling were lowered over the kitchen, the sense of shelter would be intensified, but in this home one of the key characteristics of the design is the presence of the roof shape throughout, so the architects chose to use walls and vertical elements instead.

Decorative roof trusses on either side of the dining area distinguish the space from the kitchen and living room. The ceiling shape defines the "rooms," without the need for separating walls.

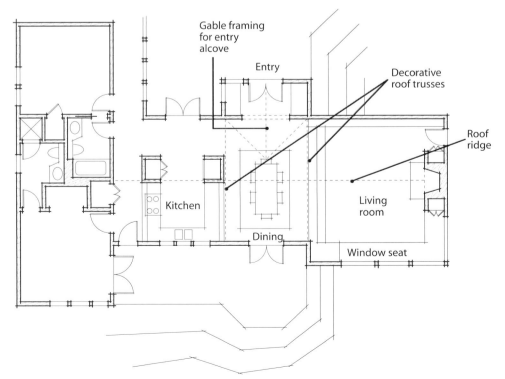

PICTURE THIS

The ceiling in this bedroom is relatively tall, but the bed is given a strong sense of shelter with the implied walls and ceiling of the four-poster bed. Without the posts, the bed seems out of scale.

The window seat in the living room is naturally sheltered by the low edge of the roof form. The flanking wall of the fireplace (at left) provides a place to lean.

At the far end of the living room, adjacent to the fireplace, there's a sheltered sitting place, a **window seat** that's nestled under the lowest edge of the sloping ceiling. Here you can lean against the flanking wall and look out at the panoramic views that surround the house. If the window seat were in a taller space, it would not have the same cozy feel and would be less appealing as a result. As we saw in the window seat described on p. 30, the more it is enclosed with walls and ceiling the more sheltered it will feel. In this instance, the architects wanted the window seat to function as part of the primary seating for the room, so they chose not to enclose it, making it more public and not intended for only one person.

The master bedroom contains an interesting example of a sheltered place within a taller, more open room. A four-poster bed creates an implied room all on its own. In times gone by, it would have been draped with heavy fabric to fashion a small warm enclosure in an otherwise drafty home. But even without the fabric, you can immediately perceive the sense of shelter provided by the four posts and their adjoining beams. Although this bedroom might feel a bit tall, making the sleepers feel unprotected, the four-poster scales down the area, providing a more intimate space.

The last sheltered place in the house is in fact a separate structure—a small studio retreat room, just big enough for one or two people. In the photo shown on p. 28, you can clearly see that the shape and slope of the roof strongly affect the sense of shelter. They define and protect the room much as a hat defines and protects its wearer.

Because this entire house expresses the shape of the roof on its interior, using it to determine the ceiling shape in each room, you could also say that the roof form creates a sense of shelter around all the activities taking place within the house. In many ways, this is the ultimate sense of shelter— the roof over our heads.

The Cheney House

Frank Lloyd Wright's houses are particularly rich in examples of Shelter around Activity, often with a variety of ceiling heights and alcoves to help differentiate the various activity places. In the Cheney House (1903) in Oak Park, Illinois, the partial walls and floating shelf between the two spaces clearly separate one "room" from the next, even though they are open to each other and share the same ceiling form. The ribs on the ceiling help to define and shelter the two spaces.

With its classic gabled form and well-proportioned scale, the tiny studio retreat next to the house exudes a sense of shelter.

THREE

Sequence of Places

Instead of thinking of a house as a set of rooms, it is useful to see it as a sequence of places in which the various daily activities of the household can take place.

HOUSES BUILT A CENTURY AGO were almost always comprised of discrete rooms, with only a doorway connecting one room to the next. This was appropriate when our lives were more formal, when the kitchen, now the hub of activity in most homes, was considered only a utilitarian and smelly place, best kept well isolated from main living spaces. But today we tend to live in our homes very differently. We are much more informal, and it's the norm in most households for more than one activity to be going on in a single area at the same time. For example, while someone is cooking the evening meal, others nearby are conversing, doing homework, or watching television. An isolated kitchen doesn't work well for this state of affairs.

So instead of thinking of the house as a series of isolated places connected by doors, it's much more helpful to conceptualize it as a Sequence of Places that can be woven together in all sorts of different ways. Each place needs its own borders, to distinguish it from adjacent places, but you don't always have to use separating walls to accomplish this. The walls, floor, and ceiling can be "sculpted" to tailor the shape of the space to the needs of the activities contained therein. Each place can also be linked to the next by a view, an entrance, or a wide opening. The larger the opening, the wider or longer the view, and the more pronounced the entrance, the more apparent the connection will be. Some places need strong connections between them to work together, while others work better with connections that are less pronounced, depending on the amount of interactivity desired.

By approaching the house as a Sequence of Places, all the space can start working together in an effective way.

Alcoves off a Central Space

In the previous chapter we learned that an alcove allows you to add a small amount of floor space to a room and have it serve an additional function. But you don't have to stop at one alcove. When you are designing a house as a Sequence of Places, alcoves can be very useful tools in creating room for a wide variety of activity areas of different shapes and sizes, all opening off a central space. A primary gathering spot, such as a family room or kitchen, can readily accommodate several separate alcoves.

In the example shown here, two alcoves open off a central living area that runs the full length of a house designed by architect Barbara Winslow. The stairway is configured to wrap around the woodstove and adjacent chair, creating a cozy corner off the kitchen, while a larger alcove off the living room a few steps away doubles as a fireplace inglenook and guest bedroom. The dining area and entry are also essentially alcoves off the central space (see the drawing on the facing page). Together they create a Sequence of Places that allows the rooms to serve multiple functions simultaneously, without being blocked off by separating walls.

Alcoves off Circulation

Another way to use alcoves is to create a Sequence of Places linked together by a connecting hallway or walkway. An alcove here can mean something as large as a regular room, but with one or more sides open to the hall. In this way, the house becomes less a series of rooms and more a progression of spaces.

The New England home shown here is organized in exactly this fashion. The main hall gives both a clear view of and access to each of the alcoves and activity places along its length so that the whole living area of the house appears as a Sequence of Places. Such an arrangement gives the home an open feel, yet there is still a strong sense of shelter because each area is shaped and sized to accommodate its particular activity, just as a separate room would be.

Connecting Views

For a house to really work as a Sequence of Places there needs to be a strong visual connection between areas, so that as you move through the house you are always being beckoned by the next "room" in the sequence. At the same time, as you are engaged in one activity area, you can still see and hear what is happening in adjacent areas. A connecting view can be as simple as a wide doorway or an arched opening, or it can be an opening in a wall between two spaces. You can read more about connecting views in Chapter 5, Interior Views.

Nooks and Crannies

In most homes there are some small potential living spaces that get enclosed behind studs and wallboard in the name of expedience and cost containment. But if they are developed, these spaces can add a wonderful dimension to a design and can play a distinctive role in a house composed as a Sequence of Places.

These nooks and crannies run the gamut from a pocket of space under the stairs, to a spot tucked between a closet and an exterior wall. These spaces serve all sorts of purposes. They can be used as unusually shaped desk alcoves and sitting places or to exhibit pieces of artwork.

Bubble Diagramming By naming the places we need in a home, and then arranging them in relationship to one another using a bubble diagram, we can steer clear of the limitations of enclosing each function in a separate rectangular room. Using this technique you can actually reduce the amount of space you need, while simultaneously opening up the various activity places to one another. This gives the impression of more rather than less space, because you can see more of the house at any one time.

Of course, there are still activities that are most appropriately accommodated by a standard room with a door (such as a bathroom), but by analyzing needs using a bubble diagram first, you'll quickly be able to gauge which activities are best left open to one another and which should be closed off from view or noise.

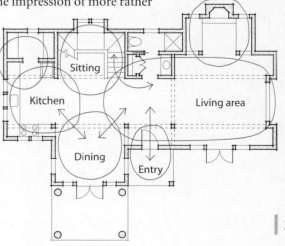

Going with the Flow

The main living spaces in this Minnesota home are organized as a sequence of places rather than as a set of separate rooms, with connecting views to adjacent spaces.

THE HOUSES that Minnesota architect Kelly Davis designs are almost always organized around a Sequence of Places rather than a series of enclosed rooms. His houses flow from space to space, with lots of **connecting views**, lots of **alcoves**, and at least a few **nooks and crannies**. The house shown here was designed for a couple and their three children. They wanted it to be a good family house but also to work well for occasions when they entertained—something they love to do.

Instead of the typical formal living room and additional family room, however, Kelly suggested a single, spacious living area that could serve both these functions, with connecting views to the kitchen and to the dining area. With the entire living space open and visible from one place to another, the house appears to be significantly larger than it actually is—one of the major advantages of designing a house as a Sequence of Places.

Looking at the relationship between kitchen, living, and dining areas, you can clearly see that although each "room" is well defined with the use of floating shelves and partial walls, there are strong visual connections between them. Essentially, both dining room and kitchen are **alcoves off a central space**, and the breakfast area is an alcove off the kitchen. Someone working in the kitchen has good visual access to activities in the

The sequence of places continues outside the home, with several decks that extend the living space into the landscape.

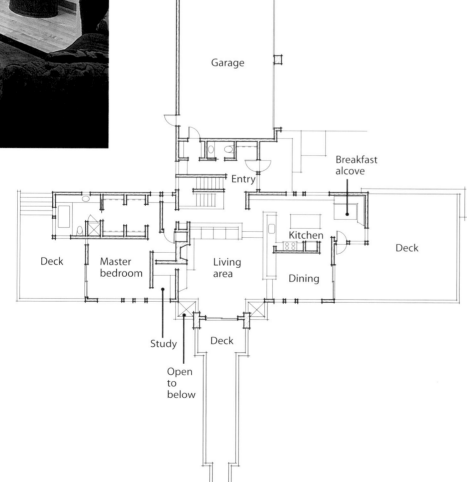

Garage

Entry

Breakfast alcove

Kitchen

Deck

Deck

Master bedroom

Living area

Dining

Study

Deck

Open to below

The kitchen is clearly a separate space, differentiated from the living room by a set of floating shelves, but there's a strong visual connection that allows the two rooms to work together.

The breakfast nook, an alcove off the kitchen, continues the Sequence of Places and opens onto one of the house's three decks.

The dining room is designed as an alcove off the central space, but like the kitchen it is also given definition with the continuation of the floating shelf and a partial wall that screens the buffet from view.

living area but from the living room it's not possible to see the kitchen prep area, because of a two-step difference in height between the two rooms, as well as a raised countertop that screens the countertops from view. This is a feature that is highly desirable for many cooks, who like the idea of an open view between kitchen and living areas but have concerns about the visibility of food prep, pots, and pans. The same raised countertop extends through to the dining room to provide a partial screen when everyone is sitting down to a meal. Yet you can still see from the fireplace end of the living room all the way to the far corner of the dining room—a view of some 36 ft. in length. If

the spaces were enclosed, your eye would be stopped by a full wall, making the rooms seem small. It's the length of the view from place to place that creates the illusion of increased space.

The informal eating area, with its lowered ceiling, and bench seating tucked in behind the adjacent cabinetry, is a wonderful example of a small alcove that's been added onto a larger area—in this case the kitchen—to accommodate a second activity. The area is defined by the floating shelf that runs between the two spaces (for more about floating shelves, see p. 47). Because it's above eye height it doesn't limit the view in any way, but it obviously indicates that this is a

The house reveals its secrets gradually. From the front entry, you can see into the living room with a view that's unobstructed horizontally. But it's not until you step past the built-in couch, nestled behind the low wall seen here, that you realize the room has a vaulted ceiling.

row opening that extends all the way to the ceiling, through which you can glimpse the study beyond—another much smaller **connecting view**, but one that delights, giving just a hint that there's more to this house than initially meets the eye.

A house designed as a Sequence of Places can feel airy and open and will almost always appear to be larger than it actually is. By designing each activity area as an **alcove off the space it borders**, and by giving each one some spatial definition, either by lowering the ceiling, separating it from adjacent spaces with a floating shelf, or enclosing it to some degree with a partial wall, you can create a home that really works well for the way we live today. This kind of arrangement allows residents to interact with one another while they are engaged in all manner of different activities. No one need feel cut off or isolated. The house is perfectly designed to allow the easy and harmonious flow of daily life.

separate place. Whenever you are designing an alcove, the more you can create this kind of spatial definition, without obstructing views, the more successful the alcove will be.

Finally, there are a couple of additional alcoves in the living room that bear mention. To either side of the sliding doors to the deck are two connecting overlooks to the level below. These are enclosed with partial walls that create an alcove of sorts for the doorway. You can see this most clearly by looking at the floor plan on p. 41. To the left of the fireplace, the wall steps back a couple of feet, and Davis has used this area to tuck in a little extra storage space that's artfully designed to house the television with some display shelves above. There's also a nar-

FOUR

Ceiling Height Variety

Varying the height of a ceiling both within the same space and from room to room adds spatial interest and helps give each its own contrasting character and definition.

WHEN WE WANT TO DEFINE one space from another we typically use a wall. But once there's a wall there's also an impenetrable barrier to view and to conversation, which is not always desirable. As houses have become more open affairs, with family rooms, kitchens, and informal eating areas all combined into one "great room," there's been a loss of differentiation between activity places. Most great rooms have all three functions stuffed unceremoniously into a large rectangle of space. Ask most people who live in such spaces if this is what they really want and they'll admit it lacks a certain something. But they still don't want walls because they like the open plan—allowing easy communication from one activity place to another.

There's an alternative, however, that retains the desired openness between places, but still gives each its own definition and character. By lowering parts of the ceiling, you can sculpt the spaces to identify and define each of the activity areas within a single room.

Ceiling height variation is one of the least frequently used, but most effective tools for defining space. Although most people are surprisingly sensitive to the effects of ceiling height, many of us have the almost reflexive belief that lower ceilings are bad and higher ceilings are good. But, in fact, any ceiling that is all one height is rather boring, no matter whether it's high or low. The art of the ceiling plane lies in creating contrast—using lower ceilings for less important or more private spaces, and higher ceilings for the more important or public spaces.

Dropped Soffits

We're most familiar with soffits over kitchen cabinets or above the countertop in a bathroom. In the photo above, a 2-ft.-deep soffit runs around the circumference of the room directly above the outer edge of the countertops. It not only provides an excellent location for recessed lighting for the work surface below but also creates a sense of shelter for those working at the countertop.

The dropped soffit gives the room considerably more character and a significantly better sense of scale than if the ceiling had been left at a uniform height throughout. Although you might imagine that the lowered soffit would make the room feel smaller, in fact it has the opposite effect, emphasizing the height of the center section and making it seem taller as a result.

Lowered Alcove

The lowered ceiling of an alcove helps accentuate the difference between the smaller space and adjacent areas. Without the lowered ceiling, an alcove can still work, but it is less distinct from the rest of the room. As can be seen in the photo above, the lowered ceiling makes the alcove more nestlike—a tiny room that looks into the larger space. In this case, the alcove ceiling height is the same as that of the soffit above the kitchen cabinets, which gives the entire room a more tailored and integrated look.

Lowered Hallway

In most homes built today, the ceilings of hallways are made the same height as the connecting rooms, giving no indication of relative importance. Such hallways usually end up feeling too tall for their width, which makes them quite uninviting.

By lowering the height of a hallway that enters a primary room, the main room will seem taller than it really is. This effect occurs because of the contrast in ceiling heights. Our senses tend to exaggerate the difference between the two ceilings. This is an excellent example of compression and release. As you move through the lower hallway, you feel the compression of space. Then as you enter the taller area, there's a noticeable sense of release.

The proportions of the hallway are important. If you make the ceiling too low, or the distance between side walls too narrow, it can be uncomfortably tight. In general, I won't make hallways lower than 7 ft. tall, and I try to leave at least 3 ft. 4 in. between the side walls. A long hallway will need to be both taller and wider.

Floating Shelf

Another tool to separate one space from another is the floating shelf. This can be used in much the same way that you would a soffit, except that it is open above, which means it can also double as exhibit space or as a light cove. When a floating shelf spans across open space, as it does in the home shown here, you can clearly see how effectively it delineates one "room" from another without any obstruction of view. If a soffit had been used here, there would be no view to the higher ceiling area.

Ceiling as Sculpture

While it is least expensive to make a flat ceiling, if you have the budget, you can create all sorts of wonderful effects by using the ceiling surface as a form of interior sculpture. In the bedroom shown here, the ceiling has been lowered at the edges, and beautifully curved to form a modified barrel vault. The form is accentuated with the double line of trim every 4 ft.

Ceiling Height Hierarchy

You can also use ceiling height to identify which space is the most important in a room and which is subordinate to it. The photo above shows a study that opens off a master bedroom. It has a lowered ceiling, which is a continuation of the shelf above the windows in the main space. The shelf and the study ceiling are a little like the lid of a box, and the space below is clearly smaller and less dominant than the adjacent vaulted-ceiling area.

Implied Ceiling If you have a very tall ceiling, it's often desirable to give a suggestion of a lowered ceiling to increase the sense of intimacy for a particular activity area below, even though it's really an optical illusion. This can be done in a number of ways.

In the photo shown here, the light fixture above the dining room table gives a suggestion of a ceiling. One's peripheral vision picks up on it and senses that there's a "cap" over the table. The lower the fixture, the stronger the sense of cap. Other elements that can imply a ceiling include such things as beams and lattices, which you can read about in Chapter 20, Pattern & Geometry.

Defining Places

ARCHITECT MARK KAWELL uses variations in ceiling height throughout this new home in Minnesota, to create a wide variety of characters of space within a great room. If you look at the floor plan on the facing page, you'll see three primary areas—the kitchen, the dining room, and the living room. There's also a wide opening directly across from the dining room that leads to the entry foyer. If all this floor area were at one ceiling height, the space would be monotonous. Each space would have more or less the same character. But by working with the three-dimensional space, raising the ceiling in the most important areas and lowering it around the edges, a dynamic and much more differentiated design results. The ceiling height variations give the appearance of separate rooms without the introduction of separating walls.

A long ridge runs the length of the room from the living area toward the kitchen, with

The ceiling heights in this home are designed to indicate the relative importance of each space. The areas beneath the primary vaulted ceiling seen here are the dominant rooms—the living room and kitchen. Subordinate rooms are separated from this main space by a continuous floating shelf that runs the length of both sides.

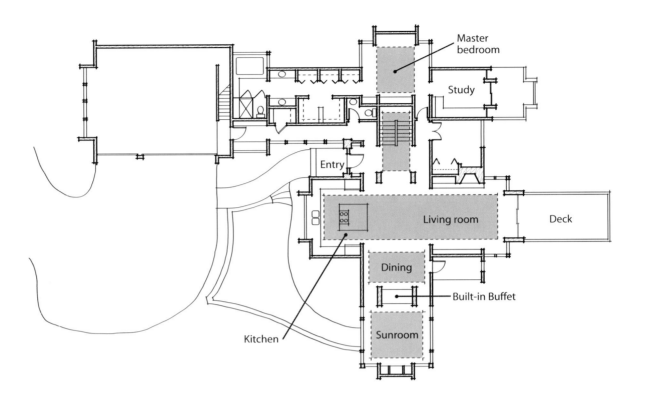

Master bedroom

Study

Entry

Living room

Deck

Dining

Built-in Buffet

Kitchen

Sunroom

another ridge intersecting at right angles to create cathedral ceilings over both the dining room and the foyer. In most contemporary homes, this would be the extent of the height changes, with the ceiling essentially following the roof form. Ceilings like these can look impressive, but they aren't particularly comfortable to sit beneath, because the focus of the room becomes the vaulted form rather than the activity area below. What Kawell has done beyond this is introduce an additional ceiling element—a **floating shelf** that runs at a height of 8 ft. from the floor all the way along both sides of the room. This transforms the area into much more defined rooms and a much more comfortable living space. The shelf also

The lowered hallway and the floating shelf above the kitchen cabinets keep the spaces human scaled. If the shelf were removed, the kitchen and hallway would seem monumental—more suited to a public building than a house.

Feature lighting added below the floating shelf creates a tiny art alcove with a lowered ceiling.

Lowered hallways connect vaulted rooms throughout the house, which emphasizes the sense of importance of the taller rooms.

offers the eye something to rest on that is more human scaled. Without the shelf, the emphasis of the space would be on height alone. With the shelves in place, the focus is brought down to the area below it and to the activities of the rooms themselves.

At the dining room, the shelf sails across the opening between it and the living area, creating a gateway that marks the edge of the room and gives a strong sense of entry. The same thing happens at the other side of the great room, where the grand piano is located, as the main room opens into the foyer.

In the kitchen, the shelf becomes the top cap for the kitchen cabinetry as well as an excellent location for task lighting for the counter space below. And in the living room, the shelf provides intimate areas on both sides of the room, below which artwork is displayed. At either corner, a pair of windows dissolve the hard boundary of the wall surfaces, giving the impression that the space below the shelf extends out into the garden beyond. Throughout all these spaces the shelf also contains cove lighting, which casts a beautifully warm indirect lighting for the entire area during evening hours.

Hallways and less important rooms, such as the study and the master bedroom closet are at the same 8-ft. height as the shelves in the living room, whereas more dominant spaces, such as the master bedroom itself, are vaulted like the living area. In fact, if you look closely at the plan, you'll see that the 8-ft. **shelves, soffits, lowered hallways,** and subordinate rooms form a layer of the house. The vaulted ceilings are revealed only where this 8-ft. ceiling layer is carved away.

The Kimball Art Museum

Architects use Ceiling Height Variety a lot in the design of public places, as well as in private houses. Now that you're familiar with the concept, look around as you visit public buildings, such as schools, libraries, and office buildings, and you'll see it employed with amazing frequency.

In one of my favorite buildings, the Kimball Art Museum in Fort Worth, Texas, architect Louis Kahn used lowered ceiling areas to flank the primary gallery spaces, which are flooded with light from specially designed window spines above. Not only do the darker lowered areas create a pleasant contrast to the taller bright middle space but the sense of being in a sheltered area of quiet remove is palpable. That is the direct result of the lower ceiling areas, which surround each gallery with a protective moat of space.

Secondary rooms, like the study off this master bedroom, have ceilings at the same height as the hallways, which gives the impression that the 8-ft. ceiling plane has been peeled away in the more important rooms to reveal the vault above.

FIVE

Interior Views

When we think about the views offered by a house, we are normally referring to exterior views, but carefully designed interior views can also add enormously to the quality and character of a home.

IN MOST HOUSE PLANS, the primary design considerations have to do with function and spatial adjacencies—which room is next to which. But there's another, equally important, level of architectural design that focuses on visual composition. Like a beautiful piece of music, a really well designed house engages us in its rhythms and melodies and provides inspiration from each of its various activity places for eye and heart alike. Many of the houses featured in this book are composed in this way. There's a harmony that's readily apparent, though not always easy to describe.

There are, however, some basic strategies that architects and interior designers often employ as they go about composing an interior layout that will help explain what makes these houses so engaging. All these strategies have to do with revealing part but not all of what's present in the house, so that the imagination is stimulated. One of my favorite examples to illustrate this principle is the photo on the facing page. Standing at the doorway, you can see all the way through the house to the kitchen at the far end. But you don't see everything from this vantage point. You are given a partial view of the dining area, which builds anticipation and makes you want to explore further.

As you look through the photos in this book, you'll notice that many of them are captivating because the space has been designed to involve your imagination, to lead you through to the next activity place, and the one beyond that. Your participation is invited at every step and from every resting place. Just as a good book makes you eager to turn the page to learn what happens next, a well-designed house beckons us to turn the corner to see what's there.

Diagonal Views

In basic geometry, you learned that in a right-angled triangle, the longest line is the hypotenuse, which connects the two perpendicular legs. In most houses, the side and front or back walls of the house are equivalent to the perpendicular legs of the triangle, and the hypotenuse is the connecting line between the two ends.

One of the most effective ways to make a small house seem larger and more engaging is to open up a view from one corner of the space to the opposite corner so that you are able to look directly along the hypotenuse, creating a diagonal view, as shown here. The house remodeling shown here was designed to do exactly this. Although the rooms are small, the open walls of the central living room allow you to see through to the spaces beyond. Here we are looking from the far corner of the library to the kitchen eating area at the opposite corner.

Long Views Through

In a long house, you can open up the view through the space from one end to the other to make the house feel bigger than it actually is. Unlike a basic connecting view, where you are simply linking one space with the next, the long view through is usually an alignment of multiple connecting openings and pass-throughs, or a view along a continuous walkway that stretches from one end of the house to the other. As can be seen here, the long view through often allows a glimpse or two of the Sequence of Places along the way. As with the partially hidden view, a long view through tends to draw your attention to the next space and the one beyond that, encouraging you to explore the house further.

Connecting Views

A room on the main level of the home that can't be seen easily from the primary living spaces, is not likely to be used much. It's as though you forget it's there. This is a common problem in many homes, where the formal living spaces in the house—the living room and dining room—are isolated from the kitchen and eating area, with only a doorway connecting them. To make these separate spaces more useful, and more a part of the everyday living space, it's important to make an opening or two in the walls that separate them, creating some connecting views. Once a space can be seen, you'll start to use it.

In the house shown here, the opening between the kitchen and the dining and living areas means that whenever someone is working in the kitchen, he or she can see through to the formal spaces. Without the opening, there'd be no visual connection and no easy way to communicate between the two. A connecting view makes the house feel more open, and the interior views are more attractive because of the visual variety.

Partially Hidden Views

An effective way to make a view more intriguing is to give just a glimpse of a room or activity place, without showing all of it. This engages the eye and makes you want to explore, to find out what's around the corner. Although the people who live in the house already know what's there, it still evokes the same physiological response. It reminds you that the space is there and it draws you in. There's a sense of mystery.

Both the houses shown here apply this concept very successfully. In one, there's a room hidden behind the fireplace that's partially visible from the main entrance into the living room. You can feel the pull to explore from this view. In the other house, there's a cutout in the floor of the living room that offers a glimpse of the level below. Although you can see very little—only the corner of a couch and a couple of items on the windowsill—it tells you enough that you'd like to know more.

Surprise Views

Although we tend to want to flaunt every beautiful view in a house for all to see, a particularly unique view can often have a more powerful impact if it is revealed only in a place where it isn't expected. The "surprise view" shown here, through a low opening between a kitchen countertop and upper cabinets to pieces of art in the living room beyond, is visible only as you bend down to peer into this unusual pod of space. When standing up straight, you can't see through. All you see is the countertop and a glimpse of the lower part of the kitchen. You'll learn more about "Pod of Space" in Chapter 12, Differentiation of Parts.

The Art of Interior Views

THIS HOUSE WAS DESIGNED for a couple approaching their retirement years by architect Eric Odor, of SALA Architects in Minneapolis. It sits on a bluff overlooking a large lake in Wisconsin and offers a wonderful example of how Interior Views can be used to make a relatively small and very simple house seem both larger and more interesting. If you look at the floor plan, you'll see that the main living space, which includes kitchen, dining, living, and music areas, is a basic square, just 28 ft. wide. Because it is so open, with only one small segment of wall separating the kitchen from the piano alcove, there are four primary **diagonal views** available, one from each corner.

Despite the simplicity of the space, no two views look alike though they are clearly related in style. The variety has been created with the use of a few well-placed ceiling features that help define each activity place and add personality to the overall design. It's the wood beams, the fir plywood ceiling in the hallway, and the floating light shelf that make this simple layout work functionally and look beautiful at the same time. All these ceiling elements divide the space into distinct activity areas, without ever obstructing the views between them.

There are also a couple of **long views through** the space as well. Standing in the main entry, adjacent to the front door, you have a clear view of the entire length of the house to the far end of the living room. With a wood ceiling to define it and a window at either end, this central walkway seems to extend beyond the limits of the walls of the house. If in your mind's eye you

The floating light shelf and the overhead beams that define the central hallway add interest to the long diagonal view from the kitchen to the dining room.

The floor plan for this house is just a simple rectangle, but the wide variety of connecting views from one place to another makes the experience of the interior just as pleasing as the views through the windows.

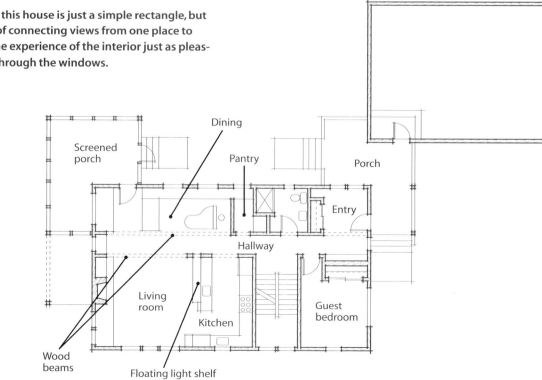

Screened porch

Dining

Pantry

Porch

Entry

Hallway

Living room

Guest bedroom

Kitchen

Wood beams

Floating light shelf

cover up the window at the end of the walkway, you'll see that the house seems to retract in length. It's the light at the end of the axis of view that has the greatest impact on increasing the apparent length of the house.

Although the main living area is almost entirely open, it contains an example of a **connecting view,** which is applied a little differently from what would be done in a house of separate rooms. Whereas a connecting view usually offers the only visual link between two activity places, in this house there is a **surprise view** in the wall segment between the kitchen and the piano alcove, and it is used here to frame a view to the piano for someone sitting at the kitchen island. Surprise views like this can add a lot to the character of a house. An Interior View doesn't have to be practical, its design can also be playful.

And, finally, there's also a **partially hidden view,** though again one that is unusually applied. Just behind the piano alcove and across the walkway from the kitchen there's a walk-in pantry. Instead of building the colored wall all the way to the outside surface of the house, it stops short, aligning with the front face of the cabinetry. This creates a partial view from the piano alcove to the window in the pantry and the

space beyond while the rest of the room is concealed from view. This gives the sense that space is flowing through and around the piano alcove without being completely contained by the walls that surround it.

What's most remarkable about the living area is that the interior views are so beautifully composed and crafted, with the introduction of a minimum of additional design features. Most of us would never think of placing a full-height wall with an opening in it at the end of the kitchen island, yet without the wall there'd be far less spatial definition and less interest for the eye. Each of

From the entry, a long view through the house draws us in. With a window at the far end and beams and wood-veneered ceiling overhead, the view is also defined as a central hallway.

A section of wall at the end of the kitchen counter partially conceals what lies beyond, but an opening allows a connecting view. Without the wall, the entire living area would seem plain and static.

the views would be less engaging. The exposed beams along the walkway could have been hidden in the ceiling, but by allowing them to be seen and by adding the fir plywood between them, the beams lend a lot of visual interest and help to organize the space. Furthermore, the light shelf implies a ceiling above the kitchen island and piano alcove, which makes them seem a little more sheltered and more private, even though they are wide open to the rest of the space. This is the art of the interior view—making small additions to the basic necessities of the space to add visual interest and personality.

The brightly colored wall behind the piano stops short to provide another partially hidden view and a glimpse of the room beyond. From here you can't tell what it is, which makes the view more intriguing.

SIX

Layering

By delineating one activity place from the next with layers of structure or other visual cues, a space can be made to appear significantly larger than it actually is, as well as more visually appealing.

WHEN COMPOSING A SENTENCE, the writer breaks it into phrases, separated by commas, to make it easier for the reader to grasp the meaning. In architectural design, the same kind of technique is used to make a space interesting and understandable.

For several years I collected magazine photos of house interiors that particularly appealed to me. I noticed over time that there was a quality to these homes that attracted me, namely a Layering of visual and spatial information. Whether this Layering came about because I was able to see from one place to another and to another beyond that, or whether it was because of a structural form like a series of posts and beams, my senses seemed to respond positively. The layers helped me understand the spaces, much like punctuation clarifies a sentence. Take away the defining layers and each space would have been much less engaging.

In a standard house composed of rectangular or square rooms, the walls are in effect layers, but because we can't see through them anywhere except at a doorway, we don't perceive them as such. But open up the walls so that you have greater visual access to the space beyond, and suddenly the walls turn into a penetrable membrane between two separate places. It is then a visual layer.

In the photo on the facing page, the pattern created by the structure divides the space into discrete places, while only minimally obstructing views. The posts and beams, which are essentially implied walls, create the layers of information available to the eye.

Framed Openings

Framed Openings in Series

When you want to make a clear distinction between one room and the next, but you don't want something as impenetrable as a wall, one option is to use a framed opening. In essence, a framed opening is nothing more than a wide doorway, that has no doors to close it off.

A standard doorway is typically only from 2 ft. to 3 ft. wide, so it doesn't give you much visual connection between the spaces on either side. Widen that opening to 4 ft., 5 ft., or 6 ft., however, and you have a much stronger connection. You can easily see into the adjacent space, and the woodwork surrounding the opening acts like a picture frame, focusing your attention on the view beyond. We are most familiar with this application in older homes such as those in the Bungalow or Victorian style, where the living room and dining room are typically separated by a framed opening of some sort and are often cased with a wide band of wood trim on either side.

The best example to illustrate the principle of Layering is a series of framed openings. In the photo above, it's as though the house were made up of multiple layers of surfaces that in turn contained the spaces between. Very much like punctuation, a series of framed openings helps us understand what we are seeing and experiencing spatially. Each framed opening defines one surface layer, and as you look through from one to the next to the next, the house becomes more intelligible because the eye is given information about how the space is assembled and organized.

Connecting Pass-Throughs

A connecting pass-through between two rooms or spaces is similar to a framed opening, except the opening that makes the connection doesn't go all the way to the floor. So it's an opening for looking through, not for walking through. When we can see from one place to the next through an opening in a wall we are looking through a surface layer and are connected visually and acoustically to what is happening on the other side. Without the connecting views, both of the kitchens shown here would be much more isolated, and anyone working in either would be unable to take part in the activities going on in the adjacent living spaces.

Arcade

An arcade is a covered walkway defined by columns on one or both sides. The row of columns forms an implied wall, though one that is so loosely defined that there's almost no obstruction to view.

It's interesting how often people will object to the idea of including even one column in a design, let alone several, because they are afraid of blocking the view. What isn't understood is that the columns actually support the structure above so that there's no need for a solid wall in their place. This means that there's far greater visual connection between adjacent spaces. In addition, an arcade creates a sense of Layering, which makes the space it defines both more interesting and apparently larger than it really is because of the additional visual information.

Implied Walls

Sometimes, instead of a completely solid wall, it's desirable to have a suggestion of a surface layer without creating a complete barrier to sound and view. In other words, there's an implication of a wall that's really a fairly permeable membrane.

Looking at the wood screen shown above, you'll see that from the bedroom side there's a definite sense of boundary. Although you can see through it, there's no question that the screen defines the edge of the stair platform and gives a sense of enclosure to the bed area. From the hallway side, however, the screen is simply a filter for the view. It obscures the view slightly, but doesn't block it. In general, the more obscuring the screen or lattice to sound and view, the stronger the sense of boundary will be, and the boundary will always feel stronger the closer you are to it.

Sliding Partitions

It's also possible to open and close a layer of wall surface, for example with a sliding door, screen, or partition. Whenever there is a need for a space to be open on some occasions and closed on others, a sliding partition is a useful tool. It's a layer that can literally disappear when necessary.

You may want to have a room open to another most of the time but occasionally need to hide it from view. This is often the case between a kitchen and dining room, for example. When open, the sliding partition is hidden away, either within a wall pocket or nested against an adjacent wall (as shown here), taking up no floor space and all but disappearing. But when closed, it completely conceals the space beyond. A sliding partition can provide a barrier to view and, if made of a substantial material, can reduce or eliminate the acoustical connection between spaces as well. (You can read more about sliding partitions in Chapter 10, Openability.)

Opening Up the Walls

THIS LITTLE HOUSE designed by architects Ralph Cunningham and Lee Quill was remodeled in 1997 and transformed from a set of conventional rooms into an engaging Sequence of Places, separated from one another by a series of framed openings that define each room but still allow numerous connecting views between them. If you look at the before plan on p. 66, you'll see that the kitchen and bathroom were relocated to create a better entryway and overall layout, but the other rooms remained in their original locations. The living room used to be far more enclosed and much darker than it is now, and views to other spaces were limited to the three doorways. The architects saw an opportunity to make the house appear larger and significantly more dynamic and light filled by opening up the walls of the living room so that wherever you stand in the main level of the house, you can see through this central space to the rooms beyond.

Instead of leaving the wall just one stud thick, they increased the depth so that some of the openings can be used to display art. The wall between the living and dining areas is a full 2 ft. thick, and its **framed openings** are used to display a collection of pots and vases. The wall's thickness

In this remodel, the framed openings between the dining room and the living room constitute an implied wall—one that's partly solid, partly open.

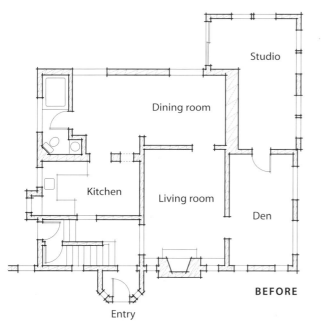

Sliding partitions allow the kitchen to be opened or closed from view. When open, there's no obstruction to conversation or view, but when closed, it's as though the kitchen no longer exists. The room is isolated from the others.

Antique stained-glass panels create a semi-permeable layer between living room and library.

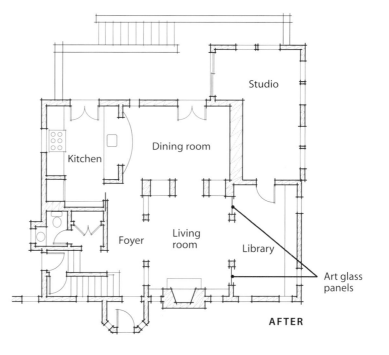

BEFORE

AFTER

Entry

When the pocket door between the kitchen and the foyer is open, you can see through three layers of structure: the wall containing the door, the implied wall defining the edge of the foyer, and the stained-glass panel wall separating the living room from the library.

reduces the visual connection somewhat but still allows many glimpses through to the adjoining space. In general, the thicker the layer that you are looking through, the more spatial definition there is for the spaces on either side. The walls on the other two sides of the living room are not as thick and have been used on one side for narrower display shelving and on the other to frame two pieces of Victorian art glass. The framed glass panels function as **implied walls**, obscuring the view through to the library beyond but still allowing natural light from the library's windows to penetrate into the living room.

From within the living room itself, the three walls form an **arcade** of sorts, so that you can see through to all the adjacent spaces, yet still have a strong sense of enclosure and containment. And from any of the surrounding spaces you can see through layer after layer of interior wall surfaces to the exterior wall beyond.

There's one final layering technique that has been implemented in this home—a pair of **sliding partitions** above the eating counter in the wall between the kitchen and dining room and another **sliding door** between the kitchen and foyer. When these sliding doors are open there are wide connecting views to the adjacent rooms, and someone in the kitchen can participate in conversations occurring in either the dining room or the living room. But when closed, the kitchen disappears, hiding the sounds, sights, and smells of food preparation.

SEVEN

Inside Outside

By conceiving of the house and the surrounding landscape as a single integrated whole rather than as two separate environments, there will be a constant interplay between the natural and the man-made, and between inside and outside.

Have you ever noticed that most houses are situated on their lots rather like vehicles that have landed from outer space? Even if there's landscaping surrounding the house, there's often little or no consideration given to whether any of this can be seen from the interior. Windows are generally located in the middle of the wall of each room, and no one has ever stopped to think about the quality of the view from within the space.

Most of us love to feel connected to nature and benefit greatly from access to daylight and to the beauty that springs abundantly from living vegetation. But to imbue our homes with these Inside Outside connections, it's best to design both environments together, if possible, arranging windows, doors, decks, porches, and terraces to take advantage of the key features of the evolving landscape. If there's a special tree on the property, for example, this may become the inspiration for a long view through the house and may even suggest the orientation and layout of the house on the lot.

Working with an existing home, you can design the surrounding landscape features to be seen from the main sitting places in the house, either through existing windows or by adding windows and doorways. And if you are planning a new home for a nondescript lot, then both landscape and building may be crafted from scratch to provide carefully composed views from all the major walkways and sitting places of the house.

Just as you are learning in this book to craft the space of the home's interior, the same can be done with outside space—the surrounding landscape. When both inside and outside work hand in hand, the result is a home that extends far beyond its actual walls.

Continuous Surfaces

One of the most effective ways to connect inside and outside is to blur the distinction between interior and exterior space. One technique for doing this is to continue a surface material, such as the wall, the flooring, or the ceiling, so that the eye is led to believe that there's nothing separating what's outside from what's inside. In the example shown above, the architect has continued a pattern of ceiling joists from the interior of the house to the exterior, where they are used to support a lattice of wood strips that serve as a sunscreen.

In the photo on p. 68, the windows of this house are metal, which allows their frames to be minimal. This helps convince the eye that there's little difference between inside and out. But what reinforces the illusion is that the stone walls that the windows abut continue on both sides without any interruption. The flooring is the same material inside and out as well, with only a tiny change of elevation to keep water from entering the home. It's these continuous floor and wall materials that make you believe that inside and outside are one.

Almost Frameless Windows

The closer a window is to its adjacent perpendicular wall, the more it will seem to disappear. It becomes simply a see-through membrane that separates the inside air from the outside air, while hardly restricting the view at all. The window in this window seat has no frame around it other than the narrow sashes and the mullions dividing one pane from the next. Because it hugs both the outer walls of the window seat, as well as the ceiling surface, the view seems almost a part of the room when seen from a distance, as here.

From the window seat itself, you feel as if you are sitting on a perch that is essentially outside, except for the invisible glass surface. If instead the window had been set into the wall surface, as shown in the drawing above, the experience both from a distance and from up close would be very different, and the sense of separation between in and out would be much greater.

Outdoor Focus

Whenever you can locate windows to take advantage of a special exterior view, you strengthen the connection between inside and out. When building from scratch, you may be able to locate a particular set of windows to focus on an exceptional feature of the site, like a tree or a long vista. But you can also design an exterior feature to become the focus of a primary view through the house. This was the strategy used in both the examples shown here.

The house shown above was designed around an interior courtyard, and this set of windows is located to take full advantage of the beautiful view. In the house shown at right there is a long run of stairs from the street level up to the main living level. This is the view that greets you at the top of the stairs—a serene water feature that lends visual tranquility and the gentle sound of falling water when the doors are open.

Outdoor Room

We usually think of rooms as features of the inside of the home, but we can think of exterior spaces as rooms too. When a house has a strong Inside Outside connection, there will almost always be an outdoor room or two. A "room" is really any space that has walls to define it, but the walls don't have to be made of studs and wallboard. An outdoor room may have walls of hedgerow and a ceiling of branches. And just as with interior spaces, the better defined the outdoor room, the more successful it will be.

Another very popular type of outdoor room is the screened porch. Unlike a sun room, which is an interior space enclosed by windows, the screened porch allows the unobstructed movement of air, and full access to all the sights and sounds of the surrounding landscape. The only thing separating you from the outdoors is a thin layer of screen and the roof above, so you really feel outside. The more sides of the porch that are screened, the more "outside" you will be.

Blurring the Line

This hilltop home has a wonderful inter-play between interior and exterior spaces.

Every view out from the two connected buildings has been carefully composed as an extension of the interior experience.

THIS BEAUTIFUL HOME, which contains many features characteristic of tradi-tional Japanese residential architecture, perfectly exemplifies the principle of Inside Outside. In Japan, the home is thought of as a combination of both interior and exterior space, and this house was designed in just such a fashion. Located on a hillside atop the Pescadero Mountains in northern California, the property is both secluded and serene, with a distant view to the ocean in one direction. Because the land is very steep, the struc-ture is actually composed of two separate build-ings, one containing the main living areas and the other, the higher of the two, containing the master bedroom suite and study. Although it's not appar-ent from the images shown here, the two buildings are connected by an interior stairway.

As you can see from the photo at right, both structures are surrounded by carefully crafted landscaping that gives every interior space a gar-den view. The trees, shrubs, and rocks are located closer to the house structure than would be typical in a standard American home, but this technique is particularly effective at bringing the outside in. From every window you look into a lush and sun-dappled tableau of great beauty. Large sliding doors open onto an interior courtyard that forms an **outdoor focus** as you move through the house.

Almost frameless windows stretching from the tub surround to the ceiling and wrapping around the corner give the bathroom an outdoor focus.

The outside walkway is separated from the inside by a series of sliding glass doors, which, when open, almost completely dissolve the boundary between the two.

The sliding door extends all the way to the left-hand wall, so that it appears almost **frameless**, washing the perpendicular wall with light and minimizing the boundary between inside and out in the process.

In the master bathroom, the windows surround the tub in a corner configuration and are quite large, descending below the edge of the tub platform and again creating the illusion of no boundary. At the far end of the tub, the window is actually composed of glass slats (a jalousie window) so that there's also the possibility of opening the room up to the breezes and giving the bather the sense that he or she really is outside rather than in. From this vantage point, you can also look along the deck that runs the length of the house and glimpse one of the long views to the ocean beyond. As in a number of places throughout the house, when the sliding glass doors flanking the walkway are open you can look outside or inside and through to the view, which gives the sense that the structure is more akin to a porch than a solid-walled house.

Although most locations don't offer the flexibility of the benign California climate, the art of blurring the boundary between inside and out doesn't depend on the weather. Even if this home were in a colder region, and the windows and sliding doors were not open during every season, there would still be a very strong connection between the interior spaces and the surrounding landscape.

The edge of the door is butted right up against the adjacent wall, making it appear almost frameless.

EIGHT

Changes in Level

One of the most obvious ways to differentiate one activity area from another is to either raise or lower the height of the floor relative to surrounding spaces.

IN THE LAST COUPLE OF DECADES we've become more sensitive to the challenges posed by steps to those who are mobility impaired, but there are still many situations in which a change of level is desirable to create a particular spatial effect. The experience of ascending or descending dramatically alters your perspective. And interestingly it's not just the view from one space to another that changes. There's a psychological effect as well.

When you ascend, you are aware of rising above and looking out over the surroundings. Often this is accompanied by a sense of increased privacy and of being separated from the main activity areas. You get this sense as you climb a staircase to the bedrooms on a second floor, or as you go up a short run of steps to the front door of a house. Descending from a front walkway to the main entry is much less inviting and, in fact, often feels quite uncomfortable, as though you were going down into the underworld.

To make a descent feel inviting, it needs to open into a wider expanse of space, light, and view, so that you can see what's coming next. Stairways to basements are often unpleasant because they constrict the view and descend into darkness. But make the stairway light filled and open it into a good-size room at the bottom, and the experience is significantly improved.

Like changes in ceiling height, changes in floor height can delineate one activity place from the next without the need of walls. But with a change in floor height, there's an even more powerful spatial experience. Just a step or two's height change can create a significant distinction between places, yet someone in the higher space can still converse easily with another in the lower space.

Stairs as Sculpture

Lowered Room

The device we're most familiar with for changing levels in the home is the staircase, but we usually don't give it much thought—it's just a way to get from point A to point B. But a staircase can also be an attractive piece of built-in sculpture if we pay attention to its design. The composition of the railing and spindles, the style of the treads and risers, the way the bottom step meets the floor, and the general form of the stair have a huge impact on its character, as well as the character of the spaces it connects.

The staircase shown here is a simple and elegant design from a house by architect Peter Twombley of Estes Twombley Architects. What makes this staircase so compelling is the relative proportioning of the elements. The newel post is slightly tapered, and every other board in the closely spaced railing has a small circular hole in it. Since the stairway is one of the few necessary built-ins in a house of more than one story, why not make it something that's a work of art? It doesn't have to be complicated or expensive to be beautiful.

When you go into a room that's lower than the surrounding spaces, it's as though you've moved into a quiet pool of space. It is much like when water moves to the lowest point in a stream before settling to stillness. It tends to make you want to sit and stay a while. Because of this, one very appropriate type of space to make into a lowered room is a sitting area that is also the end point of a Sequence of Places.

When a room is lowered there are some drawbacks, however, both from a construction and an accessibility standpoint. Such a space adds structural complexity, because the floor joists that support it must also be on a lower plane than the rest of the structure. So there are almost always additional costs involved. In addition, a lowered area will be out of bounds to someone who is mobility impaired, so don't make the lowered room the only social space.

Raised Room

A room that's higher than the surrounding areas of the house has a very different feel from one that is lower. It feels more like a place of retreat—almost as though you were climbing up into a tree house, even when there's only a step or two between it and the adjacent spaces. This sense can be accentuated further when the access into the raised space is narrow and offers only a glimpse of a view into the room from other areas.

In general, a raised floor is most appropriate for a room that you want to make feel separate and meditative. The exception to this is when the raised room is really more like a platform that is wide open to and overlooking the room below. Even here there is a sense of quiet repose, but the openness between the two spaces strengthens the connection and makes the upper one less introspective.

Platforms

We've talked about alcoves in previous chapters, and we've described that by lowering the ceiling the alcove becomes more sharply defined. But there is another less commonly implemented way to create an alcove: by raising the floor. This type of alcove, typically referred to as a platform, is a raised area that is attached to a larger room. It can either overlook the main room, as here, where it can be used as an expanded window seat or even as a stage; or it can be tucked away as a more private and reclusive place, perhaps behind a fireplace or bookshelves (see the drawing below).

Although platforms are less common than alcoves with lowered ceilings, they can add a wonderfully dynamic quality to a room. For families of musicians, a platform can easily be converted into a stage, and children will find no end of ways to turn a platform into the houses and forts of their imaginations.

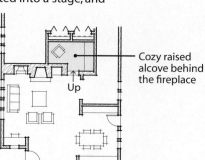

Cozy raised alcove behind the fireplace

Up

Over Under

There's something particularly satisfying about being able to see up to the second level from the main level of a house, while simultaneously looking into the space that is below this second level. Typically when we go up a staircase, we find ourselves guessing where we are located on the second floor in relationship to the spaces below. But when we can see both at once, the mystery is revealed.

If in your mind's eye, you cover up the center hallway in the photo shown here you'll get a sense of the difference. It's the fact that you can see deep into the area below the second-floor loft that makes this space so intriguing.

Keeping a Low Profile

SOMETIMES A CHANGE OF LEVEL is the only option available if you want a taller ceiling in a particular room. Such was the case in this speculatively built Los Angeles home, where a height restriction enforced by the local zoning ordinance meant that the overall house height was limited. The ordinance existed to protect surrounding houses from losing their spectacular views of downtown LA.

Because the site is steeply sloped toward the Los Angeles basin, the views from the second floor of this house are significantly more dramatic than those on the lower level. So architect William Adams, of William Adams Architects, decided to place the main living areas on the second floor rather than the first floor as would be typical. But Adams also wanted to give the living room a taller ceiling to distinguish it from the surrounding spaces, and so, since he couldn't take the roof up

any higher, he dropped the floor of the room by two steps instead. This gave it a height of 11 ft. at its center. Windows in the room come down close to the floor and extend all the way to the ceiling to give maximum exposure to the view (see the photo on p. 80).

The effect of **lowering the floor** isn't just an increase in height, however. The steps down make this **lowered room** into a distinctly separate "pool" of space. Even though there are many openings between it and the adjacent hallway,

A long skylight runs the length of the thick wall adjacent to the stairway, casting shadows that change dramatically with the time of day and the season.

The two steps down to the living room floor not only make the room taller but also signify that it is the most important space on this level.

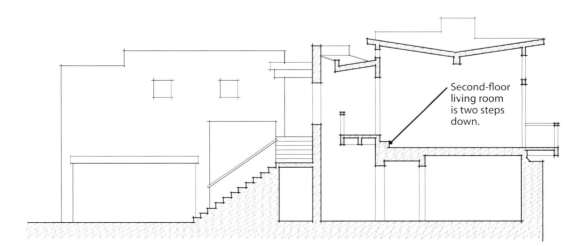

Second-floor living room is two steps down.

The main living spaces are on the second floor, which has the best views. Corner windows that extend from floor to ceiling accentuate the expansiveness of the view.

Flanked by two thick columns, the steps flow down into the living area, much like water in a stream.

there's no question where the living room ends and the hallway begins. If both living room and hallway had the same floor level, the experience would be very different. The two spaces would then bleed together and overlap.

In addition to the change of level in the living room, this house also uses its stairway to create a strong sculptural form that acts as a primary organizing device for the whole design. The stair is a straight run from the lower to upper levels and is abutted by a thick plaster wall that extends almost the full length of the house, rather like a spine. This is lit from above by a continuous skylight that casts constantly changing shadow patterns throughout the day. So the sculpture is not just one of form but also of light. The sleek metal railing adds to the sculptural quality of the stairway, its openness in stark contrast to the solidity of the thick wall on the opposite side.

Robson Square

For centuries, architects have used steps as a way to create public spaces that serve multiple purposes. The amphitheaters of ancient Greece were both bleachers for watching plays as well as wonderful gathering places. In Robson Square at the Provincial Government Centre in Vancouver, British Columbia, architect Arthur Erickson used a flight of steps that cleverly integrates a pedestrian ramp. It is a civic sculpture, informal seating, and level-changing device.

The long, massive wall is a powerful organizing feature, separating the house into two distinct parts. Looking along the wall, you can see both above and below the second-floor platform at the same time—an excellent example of "over under."

NINE

Public to Private

For a house to function properly, it must offer places for gathering together as a household, places to retreat to, to be alone in, and everything in between.

I F YOU'VE EVER VISITED a house that is entirely open, with no place to escape to, no quiet corner away from the hubbub of family interactions, you'll know that the experience is not a pleasant one. Although there are times when such a house works beautifully—perhaps when there is a party or a family get-together—much of the time it can wear on the nerves. There are times when we all need a little space.

A surprising number of newer homes today have this problem to some degree. Our houses are filled with all manner of noise generators, from TVs to stereos to computer games. With lots of cathedral ceilings, first and second levels connected by balconies, and wide open great rooms, the only place you can go to get away from all the noise is the bedroom or bathroom. Many older homes on the other hand have the opposite problem. Designed for an era when lives were dramatically more formal and the kitchen was isolated from other living spaces, these houses force activity areas apart that today we would prefer to have overlapping. Someone preparing a meal is either separated from the rest of the family, or everyone crowds into the small kitchen.

What's needed is a happy medium—a house in which the main gathering places and the kitchen are open to one another to some degree, with alcoves for associated activities and an away room, in-home office, or place of one's own separated by at least a closable door for quieter activities. A house that's designed around our needs for varying levels of privacy and publicness will be far more livable and will arguably even improve relationships among household members. It's such a simple concept, and yet we rarely recognize its importance.

Focal Gathering Place

Every household has its favorite gathering place in the home. For some it's the informal eating area, for others it's the area around the TV in the main living area, and for others it's a sunroom or porch. Since the focal gathering place is filled with people and activity more frequently than any other part of the house, there's usually a sense of vibrancy about it, and that vibrancy is contagious. So wherever the main social spot is for your household, it will work best if it is also a highly visible space. That way it can help breathe vitality into the spaces that surround it.

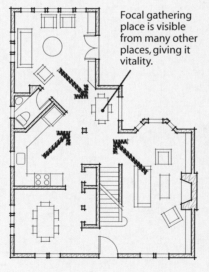

Focal gathering place is visible from many other places, giving it vitality.

   If you are designing from scratch, make sure there are clear lines of sight throughout the house to this area. And if you are remodeling, see if there are ways to open up views to this gathering place either by moving or making openings in adjacent walls.

Alcoves off Focal Gathering Place

Many families enjoy hanging out together, but not everyone wants to be doing the same thing all the time. Someone may want to read the newspaper, someone else may want to respond to some email, and a child may need to do some homework. So as well as the main sitting area in the focal gathering place, there's also a need for smaller alcoves off this primary space that can accommodate additional activities.

For example, if the focal gathering place for your family is the informal eating area, you might also want to add an alcove for a computer and desk surface. The main living area in a house works best when it allows for multiple activities in this way, so that everyone can be close but not all vying for the same seating arrangement.

   If you make a list of the kinds of activities your household might want to engage in while close to the focal gathering place, you'll probably be able to design one or two alcoves that can accommodate a variety of different secondary activities.

Away Room

If the area around the TV is usually the gathering place of choice in your household, you might want to consider adding an away room so that there's also a place for activities that require some quiet. An away room is a small room that opens off the main living area with French doors so that someone using it can still see what's happening in the other space. The doors make it acoustically separate, allowing it to be used for reading, computer work, or listening to music while the TV is on in the adjacent room. It can also double as a home office or guest bedroom.

Alternatively, an away room can function as the noise-containment room. You can close the doors, make as much noise as you want, and yet still be visually connected to the focal gathering place.

The most versatile away rooms are designed to allow for either use—quiet retreat or noise container. This can be done by including a TV in both the away room and the main gathering space, and by giving the away room a cozier, more intimate feel.

Place of Quiet Remove

Once in a while, it's desirable to have a place to go where you can be quiet and alone or where you can have a private conversation with another family member. Most homes are sorely lacking in suitable places for this kind of activity. Bedrooms are usually the closest thing we have, but they are not typically designed to accommodate a variety of functions. By adding a window seat or a comfortable chair, a bedroom can become a pleasant sitting place, and a closed door will give the signal to other household members of the desired solitude. Although this occasional need for privacy may seem rather obvious, it is amazing how little attention we pay to it when buying or building a home.

Ideally, locate bedrooms so that they are either in a private wing of the house or on a second floor. Avoid placing bedrooms directly over (or under) noisier main living areas. And if building from scratch, consider adding insulation to the walls of bedrooms and bathrooms to help minimize sound transmission. It's a simple strategy that can make the whole house a more comfortable acoustical environment.

Place of Your Own

A place of your own is a private retreat area in a home that can be used for anything from a hobby to a place to meditate. Typically, it works best if it is not a shared place but is a spot just for one person to call his or her own. It can be as simple as an alcove off a bedroom, or it can be a more isolated space like a loft or a separate studio.

Because it's unusual to include such spaces in our homes, we tend to discount the need, or try to make it work as part of another room. But if you are someone who longs for such a place, make it a priority and give yourself permission to create it. Our inner desires, whether for self-expression or for self-understanding, are important to listen to.

A Not So Little Cottage

A pass-through between the kitchen and living room serves both to connect and separate the two spaces.

THE HOUSE SHOWN HERE, designed by Dan Nepp of TEA2 Architects in Minneapolis for a single father and his two children, has a wide spectrum of places ranging from public to private. The client wanted a house that had the cozy quality of a cottage but that also had some of the hand-hewn characteristics of a mountain cabin.

Nepp understood that his challenge was to create a house that honored his client's desire for an intimate quality without it seeming small or claustrophobic. The resulting home has been masterfully designed to give a cozy feel, even though many of the rooms are spacious in terms of square footage and volume. Looking closely at the main floor, we can see how he accomplished this (see the drawing on the facing page).

The **focal gathering place** for this family is the main living area. The fireplace, as well as the TV and stereo, is located here, and large windows look out at the lake view beyond. This is the place where they hang out together, in the largest space on the main level. It can be seen from all the surrounding rooms and, with its tall ceiling and massive beams, clearly feels like the focus of the house. The dining room, which was designed to have a fairly informal character, is a focal gathering place, with a lower ceiling that falls between the main-level windows and those of the clerestory windows above. It is sometimes used for entertaining but can also do double-duty by accommodating other family activities, such as homework,

The living room serves as the focal gathering place, with views through framed openings to the kitchen and informal eating area. The thickness and solidity of the dividing wall help emphasize the separation.

games, and reading. Although it is open to the main living room, it is a slightly less public space. Someone sitting here can choose either to participate in the activities of those in the living room proper or keep more to himself and focus on the task in front of him.

To one side of the living and dining room, behind a wall that's punctured by a series of framed openings, are the kitchen and informal eating area. The wall divides these spaces from the focal gathering place but still allows sound and views to flow between. Both these spaces are less public, with lower ceilings that give them a more intimate feel, but they are still part of the public realm of the house. Without the dividing wall or the lowered ceiling, both these activity areas would become part of one large great room, and they would all have an equally public feel. To make something seem less public, you need to differentiate it from the primary space, either with a change in ceiling height or a visual separation of some kind, as with the wall of framed openings used here.

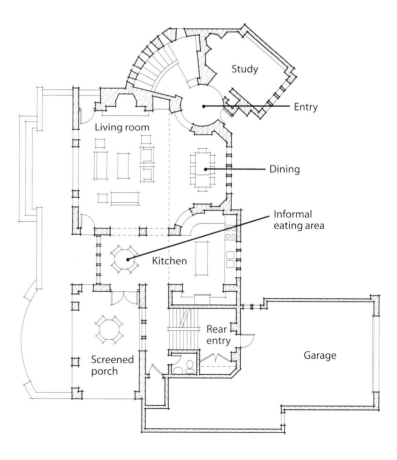

Within the essentially open floor plan, activity areas are defined by partial walls and changes in ceiling height.

The lowered ceiling differentiates the kitchen from the adjacent spaces and gives it a cottage-like feel.

Separate from the activities of the main living room, the screened porch is a more private space—"a place of quiet remove."

The big dining room table is housed in an alcove off the focal gathering place, with a lowered beamed ceiling, similar to the one in the kitchen. To the left, the study is two steps up.

Beyond the informal eating area there's another social space, the screened porch, which gains importance in the summer months. One of the biggest concerns with screened porches is how they will look in the off-season months. For this family the porch is a secondary focal gathering place in the summer, but because it is not usable for much of the year it has been placed in a less public location. It is easily accessible from all the main living spaces, but for most of the year it's hidden behind French doors that can be covered with a drape if desired, so that it's out of sight and out of mind.

On the other side of the living room, separated from the more public areas by the entry vestibule, a study space serves as a home office for the owner. The two steps up to it, combined with the size of the doorway, which partially limits the view from the living area, make it a semiprivate room that can become very private and **a place of quiet remove**, when its doors are closed. Here it is distance, elevation, and restriction of visual access that have created the sense of privacy.

Although this is clearly a house that is highly detailed and significantly more expensive than average, the techniques used to differentiate public from private spaces can be applied on much tighter budgets. Alcoves, changes in ceiling height, and framed openings don't have to cost a lot, but they can make a big difference in spatial experience and in defining the relative publicness or privacy of a space.

TEN

Openability

In most American homes, we automatically associate the concept of openability with a door or window. But there are in fact many other ways of opening and closing one space from another.

A HINGED DOOR IS A WONDERFUL DEVICE for separating one room from another, but it's by no means the only one. Yet in our culture we have made it pretty much the solo choice. Even sliding doors have a bad rap because they are usually installed with very cheap hardware that makes them awkward to open and close after a few years' use. A sliding door takes up no floor space, disappearing into the wall when not in use. With the proper hardware it will last just as long as a regular door and can be just as easy to maneuver. When used in series with multiple overhead tracks, sliding doors or screens can be designed to open a wide area. A swinging door by contrast takes up valuable floor space as it is opened and at most can be made only two door leafs wide—like a pair of French doors.

If we broaden our view of what to use to open one space to another, there are all sorts of spatial connections that we don't normally consider. The Japanese use shoji screens as much as we use doors. Rooms divided by shojis can be altered dramatically in size and in character by opening or closing the screens. So a room that during the day is part of the main living area can at night be turned into an enclosed bedroom by rolling out the bed futons.

Although our Western furnishings are too cumbersome to be moved every day, there are still many advantages to opening one space to another, as shojis and more solid panels allow. You'll see in the examples that follow that by including sliding and roll-down screens and panels into our set of spatial connecting devices, we can solve a number of common visual problems that we normally assume we have to live with.

Sliding Doors

Sliding doors, whether solid or glass, like the ones shown here, have some major advantages over their swinging counterparts. When fully open they disappear into the wall and take up no floor space. The opening between rooms appears as simply a framed opening, and most guests wouldn't even notice there were doors there at all. But when there is the need for acoustical separation, the doors can be pulled closed, and the desired quiet is obtained.

In this home, the sliding glass doors separate the kitchen from the living room and remain open much of the time. But when food is being prepared and the noises from clanging pots and pans make conversation or TV watching in the living room difficult, the doors can be shut. There's still visual connection through the glass, so the cook isn't completely isolated, but the sounds are contained.

Sliding Screens

Sliding screens, like the Japanese shojis shown here, are usually less substantial than sliding doors, but they offer some other advantages. They obscure the view between spaces when closed while yet still allow light to enter. And instead of sliding into a wall pocket, they stack one over another along an adjacent wall surface. This can add a beautiful look to the room, though it does take up a small amount of floor space.

In Japan, shojis typically run on tracks at both the floor and the top of the shoji screen. But in the West, where we aren't used to having tracks set into the floor, shojis are often simply hung from a top track. Although traditionally shoji screens were made of paper, today they are frequently made of fiberglass instead, which is significantly more durable. If you have small children, avoid the use of sliding screens until they are older, as most screens are easily damaged and not inexpensive to repair. Also, if acoustical privacy is a concern, sliding screens aren't a good choice as they do little to reduce sound transmission.

Sliding Panels

There are some locations in a house where sliding panels can be used to close off an opening between rooms, like this pass-through between a kitchen and dining area. They usually function in much the same way as sliding doors and tuck away into pockets in the walls on either side of the opening when not in use. They add a wonderful flexibility, allowing the two rooms on either side to be open or closed to one another as needed.

For a cook concerned about the visibility of dirty dishes during a formal dinner, this is a useful device that can allow one eating area to serve both formal and informal functions. In the informal situation, the panels can remain open, but when guests are over the panels can be closed if desired.

Movable Window Walls

Although in cold climates we have to make do with windows and the illusion of openness to connect us with the outside, in warmer climates it's possible to design a house with a wall of windows that can be moved out of the way so that the inside space becomes outside space when they're open. Although this is not an inexpensive option, it can create a truly wonderful experience, transforming rooms into covered porches rather than house interiors.

With the window walls closed, the room shown above has an enclosed, conservatory-like quality. It is beautiful, but it is definitely an interior space. But with the window walls moved out of the way, the experience is totally changed. There's no boundary to the "room," and it now feels much more like a park shelter and an outdoor room.

The narrow house shown at right has a series of windows on both sides that are ganged together to make large panels. These can be slid away along upper and lower tracks to open the home's interior to the outside. They work very much like interior sliding shoji screens, except that in this case the room they open into is the great outdoors.

Less into More

This tiny cottage, now used as a weekend getaway, is one of several structures that were originally designed to house families building larger homes at the The Sea Ranch in California.

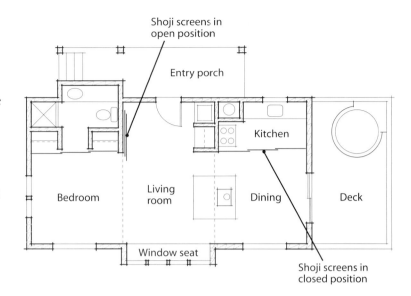

Shoji screens in open position

Entry porch

Kitchen

Bedroom

Living room

Dining

Deck

Window seat

Shoji screens in closed position

ARCHITECT FIONA O'NEILL was hired in the mid-1990s to design a series of very small speculative starter homes along the California coast in the community known as The Sea Ranch. The developer's concept was to have the cottages serve either as places to live while the purchasers were building larger homes in the area or as the beginnings of structures that could be added on to over time. It was a new proposition for O'Neill, and one that intrigued her—how to distill the designs of these homes down to the absolute essentials, making every space as multi-purpose as possible, so that the cottages could be tiny but still serve the needs of the people who bought them. Her solutions are wonderful illustrations of how one can creatively use sliding screens to make less into more—much more.

The example shown here is one of her cottage designs, which was purchased by a couple and their two teenage daughters, who use it as a week-end home. It is just 640 sq. ft. in floor area, but because of the flexibility of its spaces, it seems significantly larger and provides all the activity areas the family needs to live comfortably when they are there. (It's worth remembering, as you look at these photographs that small spaces often look bigger through the eye of the camera because a fish-eye lens is used to capture them.)

The house is made up of six primary activity areas: entry, living room, kitchen, dining area, bedroom, and bathroom. In most conventionally designed homes, the bedroom is always a bedroom and rarely gets seen or used during the day. But in this home, the shoji screens that allow the room to be enclosed and separated from the main living areas during the night can be moved out of the way completely during the day so that you can see all the way from the dining room to the

Sliding shoji screens allow this bedroom to be enclosed by night but be an extension of the living area by day (as shown on the facing page).

With shojis open, the long view through from the dining area to the bedroom makes the house seem significantly larger than its 640 sq. ft. would suggest.

With shojis closed, the house has a very different feel. It's not apparently as spacious, but the screens give the space a sophisticated elegance.

Every space is designed to accommodate more than one function. By day, the wide window seat is an extension of the living room; by night, it serves as overflow sleeping space.

windows in the bedroom at the opposite end of the cottage. The bed can then be used as an additional sitting area, essentially becoming an alcove off the main living space. There's another alcove in the living area that also does double-duty. The wide window seat that during the day is a wonderful place to sit and read or engage in conversation becomes a bed for the girls at night.

There are also shoji screens that allow the kitchen to be hidden from view if a more formal is feel desired for a dinner occasion. Though these are used less frequently than the screens covering the bedroom, their presence allows the space to undergo a significant aesthetic and functional metamorphosis; the owners simply pull the three stacked shojis along their tracks to cover the kitchen from sight.

Though we rarely use such devices in American homes, this cottage illustrates what a powerful spatial device the **sliding screen** can be. Having the ability to move a "wall" out of the way so that the space it contains is revealed can make the entire house seem significantly bigger, and more interesting spatially as well. Although sliding screens aren't appropriate for every situation, if you include them in the list of possible house components, you'll find many rooms that you've always considered static and single functioned can in fact do double-duty and be transformed with ease into totally different kinds of activity places.

Japanese Houses

Many Americans have probably heard of translucent Japanese shoji screens (made of rice paper), but they may not be aware that a traditional Japanese house also includes a number of other sliding layers that serve as barriers to the elements. Solid, sliding wood screens, called amados, protect the interior of the house from wind and rain and traditionally served as the exterior wall when closed. In today's homes, these screens also provide protection for an inner sliding window. Here, all three layers of sliding screens have been drawn back to invite the garden in.

The tiny kitchen is an alcove off the dining area. The shoji screens are stacked out of the way on the left-hand wall.

With shojis drawn across the alcove, dirty dishes are concealed and the dining area is suitable for a more formal dinner.

ELEVEN

Enclosure

*Although houses today are no longer composed entirely of discrete rooms
with highly defined boundaries, it is important to include at least a few places
that offer a greater sense of enclosure.*

IN MOST NEW HOMES TODAY we seek openness, airiness, and a blurring of the boundaries between one room and the next. We don't want to feel constrained or inhibited by the space around us. But in building homes with ever-larger volumes of space surrounding each activity, we've lost one of the essential qualities of home—a sense of Enclosure and protection. To truly appreciate the spaciousness that we hold in such high regard, we must also have places that contrast with it, places that feel contained and private.

There are, of course, different degrees of Enclosure, ranging from a small space that is completely contained with no view to a space that is defined by implied walls that allow views beyond but give a strong sense of boundary. We tend to think of a completely contained space as oppressive, and certainly it can be when poorly designed. If you think of all the powder rooms you've been into in your life—rooms that are usually fairly enclosed—there are probably some that stand out as particularly uncomfortable, and others that you found quite beautiful. It's not the Enclosure that makes them oppressive, but how the space is proportioned, how it is decorated, and how it is lit.

As we design our homes to fit our modern activities and lifestyles, there are many ways to evoke a sense of Enclosure in appropriate places throughout the house. Adding such spaces can help create some contrast to the openness of the wide-open living areas and provide a peaceful respite from the hubbub of everyday living. Whether it's a secret room, an inner courtyard, or simply a strongly defined boundary to a main living space, a sense of Enclosure can dramatically affect the quality of comfort in a home.

Containment

In the last chapter we looked at the various kinds of partitions that can be used to open and close one space from another. Now we'll look at what it feels like to be in a space that is enclosed. In the photos shown here, you see a bedroom that can be opened up to the other rooms of the house when the shoji screens are pulled back, but when they are closed it is a completely contained space, and someone using the room feels protected and secure.

The same thing happens when you close the door to a standard room. The difference between the open and closed positions is dramatic. Although the views through to the surrounding rooms are visually interesting, for someone preparing for sleep, the openness would be disconcerting. We generally want privacy and containment for those activities that we consider of a more

personal nature, like sleeping and bathing. But interestingly, there are significant differences in what people consider personal and thus what requires Enclosure. Before you design or remodel a house, make a list of the rooms that should offer complete Enclosure and make sure that you and the other members of your household are in agreement.

The Alhambra As a college student, I traveled to the Alhambra in southern Spain, a thirteenth-century citadel of extraordinary beauty. I fell instantly in love with the place and spent hours wandering the extensive grounds.

The Alhambra is literally overflowing with marvelous spatial experiences, many of them related to enclosure. Here, a large garden is hidden within the courtyard's castle-like walls. Despite the barrenness of the terrain beyond the citadel walls, these courtyards are like oases, full of vegetation and the sounds of flowing water.

Partially Hidden Room

Because the experience of Enclosure is such a powerful one, it can be used in a limited way to create a space that gives a strong sense of protection even when not a completely contained room. A partially hidden room like this library space, tucked behind a fireplace in the main living area,

is a wonderful retreat that still allows the user to hear what's going on in the primary room. It is really serving as a secluded alcove rather than a separate room.

As you walk into the living room you can't help but wonder what's around the corner and want to explore, which adds a quality of discovery that helps infuse the house with vitality. If doors were added, the sense of separation between the two spaces would be significantly increased, and an away room would be created. Both engage the experience of Enclosure, but to different degrees, and both have their place depending on the functional needs of the inhabitants.

Implied Walls

You don't have to use solid walls to create a sense of Enclosure. In fact, sometimes you can become more aware of the containment of space when there's a partial view through a wall. The dining room shown here has horizontal wood latticework on two sides of the room, one side separating it from the stairway and the other separating it from a short hallway to the study. Because you can see through these layers of implied wall to the spaces beyond, you feel at once protected from and engaged in the surrounding areas.

If the walls were solid (as shown above), you probably wouldn't think about the sense of Enclosure at all. So the implied walls serve to increase your awareness of where you are in relation to the rest of the house and actually enhance the quality of containment.

Looking Inward

Houses in hot climates are often designed to be more introverted. In this Texas home, the enclosed courtyard limits the amount of direct sunlight that enters the living space.

I F YOU LOOK AT THE FORMS of houses in hot climates around the world, you'll find that they are usually more inward looking than their cold climate counterparts, often oriented around an interior courtyard, with most of the windows looking toward this cooler, more contained and shaded outdoor space. Architect Gary Furman, of Furman Architects in Austin, Texas, employed this strategy in the house shown here, which is in a climate with often relentless sun. Designed for a couple whose children have left home, it is really a series of smaller buildings connected by walls and roofs that together combine to form an interior courtyard—a place that is almost completely enclosed, except for the opening to the sky above and the two doorways that allow you to enter.

Furman wanted to make certain that the homeowners' entry was a pleasant one and not the typical back-door experience, past or through the laundry room and other utility spaces. He placed their everyday entry adjacent to the carport and designed it to lead through a gateway in the stone of the exterior walls and into an alcove off the courtyard. A sense of **containment** is felt as you step through the solid stone walls, which heighten the sense of Enclosure. The area surrounding the gateway is shady and protected from the sun's rays, but your eye is led onward into the courtyard, a space that is light and open, though it is

At the front entry, guests are greeted first by this serene fountain set in its own tiny enclosure—a preview of the quality of the courtyard space within.

still very much an enclosed space. As you stand here, you are clearly now in the territory of the house. A covered walkway leads from here to the kitchen doorway, where you enter the interior of the house proper. So there's a gradual entry process, and all the places along the way are parts of an elegantly crafted entry transition that move you from the public world beyond the home's walls to the interior of the house.

There's a second entry for guests at the other side of the courtyard. It has similar characteristics as the homeowner's entry, and an equally gradual entry transition, but there's more of an announce-

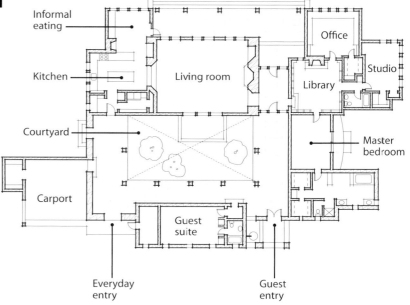

The deep greens of the vegetation give the impression of an oasis—a very different kind of environment than the dry brilliance of the home's surroundings.

The large living room windows overlook the courtyard, connecting the inner living space with the contained garden. Windows on the opposite side of the living room open onto views of a lake beyond. In effect, the room is a bridge between inner and outer worlds.

ment of arrival at the house on the exterior. A beautiful water fountain greets you as you step under the trellised arbor that links the guest suite with the main house, and a small opening in the stone wall gives just a glimpse of the courtyard beyond (see the photo on p. 103). Like the home-owners, guests are welcomed through the court-yard, and their passage into the house proceeds along the covered walkway to glass doors to the main living spaces.

Although this courtyard could have been made into an outdoor living space, Furman took his inspiration from Japanese landscaping and designed it instead to be a tranquil place to view and to enjoy from the periphery—a place to walk past, as well as to be seen from the main living areas. This house is located on a lake close to Austin, and the outward-looking living room win-dows open onto this lake view. The courtyard win-dows sit directly across from these, providing a contrasting enclosed view as counterpoint. From within the living room the effect is dramatic—a sort of yin and yang, wide open on one side of the house and sheltered and contained on the other.

The sense of Enclosure within the courtyard and surrounding walkways is so strong because you are given only a couple of small openings through which to see out. If one wall of the court-yard were completely removed, there'd be far less of the quality of containment. On the other hand, if there were no opening to the sky, the contain-ment would become an oppressive rather than a liberating experience. With any enclosure, there's a fine line between inspiration and claustrophobia.

The Bradbury Building

When I'm in Los Angeles, one of my favorite architectural experiences is to visit the Bradbury Building (famous for its pivotal role in the science fiction movie *Blade Runner*). Like many buildings of its era (1889-1893), it was designed as an office building, with each floor of offices forming a doughnut shape that opens onto a walkway surrounding a central atrium. With its huge skylight spanning the entire atrium, it is a self-contained, light-filled universe. Architect George Wyman decorated the simple form with highly ornate cast iron, giving the impression that you are enclosed in a strange sort of courtyard garden where the plants are made of metal filigree.

Four walls and an opening to the sky create a sense of tranquil remove from the world beyond the courtyard.

TWELVE

Differentiation of Parts

*To identify and express the different functions of spaces and surfaces
in a home it is often helpful to delineate or separate each element—giving
each a character that is distinctly different from what surrounds it.*

W E DRAW ATTENTION to something by delineating or highlighting it. And with this attention comes awareness of difference. Just as a picture frame focuses our attention on the image it contains, in the same way many of the applications discussed in this chapter help focus attention on the surface or object that's highlighted. Without a means of accenting one part of a surface from another, or without distinguishing one building element from another, everything becomes homogeneous and bland. Some of the homes built after World War II had this problem. All the ceilings were the same height, and often everything was finished in white, from the walls to the woodwork to the tile in the bathroom. There was nothing to relieve the monotony.

By identifying different elements with particular colors, textures, or materials, you can animate a space and help give it personality. In Chapter 6, we spoke of breaking a space into intelligible, bite-size pieces, much as punctuation does in a sentence. Differentiation of Parts serves a similar function, but with respect to objects and surfaces. There are some standard differentiations in most homes, such as flooring that's used only on the floor, not on the walls or ceiling; built-in cabinetry that's used for storage in kitchens and bathrooms; and wood trim that highlights doors and windows. But there are many other ways to differentiate the parts of a home as well.

Once you start to understand this principle, you'll see how pervasive it is, not only in house design but throughout the natural world and the built environment. In general, differentiation is the spice of life.

Exterior Beltlines

One of the most common ways to differentiate the parts of a wall surface is to create a dividing line partway up, much as a belt divides the top of the pair of pants on your lower half from the shirt that covers your upper half. In architecture, a beltline is usually created by introducing a continuous piece of trim just below the height of the windowsill and then using different materials or colors above and below that line.

In the photo above, the area below the beltline is sheathed with gray lap siding, whereas the area above is sheathed with natural wood shingles. By differentiating both the materials and the color the effect is more pronounced than if both were the same color but different materials or the same material but different colors.

Even when the materials used to sheathe the exterior are relatively inexpensive, as shown at right, with knotty lap siding above and exterior-grade plywood below, the introduction of a beltline enlivens the surface and adds immensely to the character of the house. It's one of the most effective

ways to add value to a home without spending a lot of money, provided you select cost-effective materials. If stone and brick were substituted, you would still have the differentiation of parts, but the price would be significantly higher.

Interior Beltlines

On the interior of a home we are most familiar with a beltline when it is used as the top band of wainscoting, as in this bathroom. Like the exterior examples, this beltline has been installed just below the windows, which provide the most dominant division line in the room. Sometimes there is another feature in the room that is dominant, and you may chose to make that the height of the beltline instead. For example, in this bathroom the architect might have selected to run the beltline at the height of the vanity countertop, filling in the space between the bottom of the windows and the beltline with another piece of trim.

A beltline looks best when it is run continuously around the room at the same height. Whether you add wood paneling below the line, as here, or simply use a different color of paint to differentiate the upper and lower portions of the wall surface, a beltline can add enormously to the character of any room.

Headbands

A headband serves a similar function as a beltline but is installed farther up the wall, usually above the tops of doors and windows. This is a very common feature of both Prairie School and Arts and Crafts-style homes (something that both borrowed from Japanese design). The area below the headband is often painted a different color from the area above, and the ceiling is painted and finished in the same way as the upper segment of wall. So the entire area of the room above the headband is like the lid of a box.

The room shown here has both a headband and a beltline, with three different colors to differentiate one wall surface from another. A very different effect would be created if the sequence of colors were reversed. Since darker colors tend to make the surface they are applied to seem heavier, in a smaller room I'll usually put the darkest color at the base of the wall, and the lightest at the top so that the ceiling seems taller. On the other hand, if a room is very tall, a darker color on the ceiling will give it greater visual weight and help to bring it down a bit.

Floating Surfaces

Another way to differentiate the parts of any Composition, whether it be a house, a room, or the elements of a wall surface, is to make each material appear to float separately from one another. In this kind of design it is as though each material were completely independent and had simply found a way to co-exist with the others, without merging.

An excellent example of this can be found in the living room of this Texas home where the wood ceiling seems to float above the stone side walls. The clerestory windows form a narrow band that runs much of the way around the top of the room, creating a separation between the two denser materials. These same windows are contiguous with the larger window panels below that look out over the courtyard. Unlike most rooms where the primary wall surface surrounds each set of windows and the ceiling and walls appear to be made of the same material, here the windows, the stone walls, and the ceiling are separate entities. They rest on one another, but they don't blend.

Separate Components

Pod of Space

You can also use color, texture, and shape to differentiate one component from another in a Composition. If you think about most of the raised countertops you've seen, you'll realize that they are usually designed so that the upper section, the counter surface on the kitchen side, and the backsplash that divides the two are treated as parts of a single thing. The difference in the kitchen shown here is that the raised countertop section is treated as a completely separate component that seems to rest on the lower part and doesn't extend to the far end of the island. It looks as though you could simply lift the block of wood that forms the upper section off the lower countertop, and the island would still be complete—though without a raised section.

The way that the sink is set into the countertop has the same kind of separateness. It appears to have been slid into place, with the surrounding countertop and cabinetry materials forming a container for it, but not interacting with it or overlapping it in any way.

Typically, when we want to differentiate one space from the next we'll use a combination of walls to create a room. But there is another tool you can use to differentiate the parts of a larger space. It is what I have termed a "pod of space," a freestanding element that houses an activity or storage function and that, by its presence, divides the rest of the space into distinct and differentiated activity places. A pod of space can be open above or can go all the way to the ceiling, but it is not attached to either side wall and is often, though not always, made of different materials than the rest of the room.

In the example shown here, a semicircular object in the middle of a large rectangular room houses the kitchen. It is of quite a different color and texture from the surrounding surfaces, and its placement results in the division of one room into multiple parts— a dining area behind it, where the kitchen is hidden from view, and a living area in front of it, where the kitchen becomes an open alcove.

Making a Difference

T HE HOUSE SHOWN HERE is a remodel of a previously rather bland Minneapolis home built in 1969. The remodeling was designed for a couple and their young daughter by architect Eric Odor and me during my last year at Mulfinger, Susanka, Mahady & Partners, now known as SALA Architects. Because the ceilings were 8 ft. high throughout, it was important to give the house some character by using the principle of Differentiation of Parts.

With the homeowners' encouragement, we decided to give this formerly Dutch Colonial house a Prairie-style character. Though all the exterior walls and interior spaces remained in more or less the same locations, the roof was changed dramatically, as were the interior finishes. Because Prairie houses tend to emphasize the horizontal lines running through it more than the vertical ones, creating differentiation through the use of built-ins and trim lines, this style of architecture lent itself perfectly to our needs.

The first and most prominent design change was to create a thick wall that runs the length of the house, separating the more informal side of

Formerly rather plain, this Minnesota home was transformed from a Dutch Colonial with 1950s decor into a house with a distinctly Prairie-style character.

the house, containing the entryway, kitchen, and informal eating area, from the living room and dining room. The wall is not entirely solid, allowing connecting views from one side to the other, but it is everywhere distinguished from its surroundings by its cherry coloring. Wherever you see this 2-ft.-thick wall of cabinetry, framed openings, and pass-throughs, you know that you are seeing a segment of the center spine of the house. In other words, this element of the house has been differentiated from all the rest by the material and coloring used to make it.

The original floor plan was only slightly modified, but the openness between rooms and the interior finishes were dramatically altered. Throughout the house a continuous headband defines the main wall area from the upper wall and ceiling.

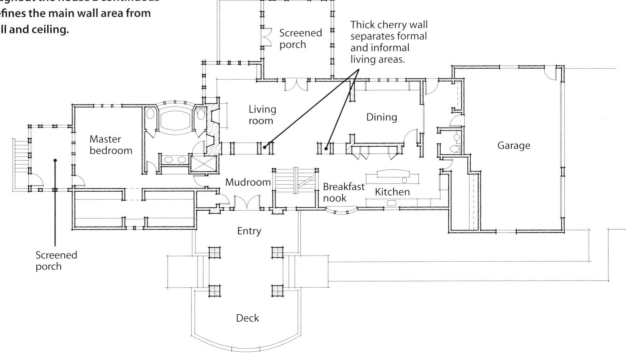

Screened porch

Thick cherry wall separates formal and informal living areas.

Living room

Dining

Master bedroom

Garage

Mudroom

Breakfast nook

Kitchen

Entry

Screened porch

Deck

Another key feature of the design is the **headband** that runs throughout the house just above the height of the window and door heads—7 ft. off the floor. By separating the area below the headband from the area above, you're given the impression that the ceiling is higher than it really is. The differentiation is further accented in many places by the use of a different color of paint above and below the line. In the photo at right, the master bedroom is given a more intimate feel with the use of a darker color below the trim band. Take away the headband and run the wall color all the way to the ceiling and the room's character is dramatically altered. Because the walls are now just one solid color, it's just like all the other 8-ft. ceilings you've ever seen. But with the trim band and the differentiation of color above and below the line, your senses perceive that there is more there.

The headband is differentiated in another way, too. In the private areas, the band is a single narrow cherry line, but in the more public areas of the home it becomes a wider two-toned band, with a maple 1x4 added above the narrow cherry band.

PICTURE THIS

If the continuous band of trim is removed and the wall paint color is extended to the ceiling, the master bedroom looks much plainer, as well as shorter.

A thick wall of cherry cabinets runs most of the length of the house and is clearly designated as a separate component.

The gentle curves of the framed openings designate important entrances between rooms—here between the living room and the foyer, stairway, and kitchen. With a maximum ceiling height of 8 ft., the curvature is limited, yet it makes a big statement.

When you use the principle of Differentiation of Parts, you can create visual cues like this throughout a design, not only to add character but also to make the house more comprehensible.

In a couple of places, the headband makes a gentle curve upward toward the ceiling, and in so doing defines an important interior gateway between zones or rooms. Even though there's only a few inches between the top of the continuous headband and the ceiling, just this small amount of curvature gives definite impact to the sense of entry. So in this home, such curves are used only where we wanted to make a statement and let you know you are entering a new zone.

One final application of this principle that's worth noting is at the stairway, which has been defined as a **separate component**. It is a block of

In the dining room, the ceiling shape follows the shape of the curved framed opening.

The stairway is treated as a separate component. Clearly of a different character than the rest of the features in the house, it appears to be held in place by the headband, which stops here, reinforcing its differentiation from other components.

space, with implied walls made of vertical cherry strips, which differentiate it from any other object or surface in the house. Where there's an important element in a design, separating it out in this way, either by using a different material, texture, or color, can make it a sculptural focal point.

Without these differentiations, this house would be just a big rambling floor plan with the standard allotment of rooms. But with the parts identified as different and separate from one another, it takes on a dramatically altered appearance and character. And it all takes place under a ceiling height that most people today believe to be "boring." This house makes it clear that the monotony isn't to do with the constraints of the ceiling height, but with the lack of differentiation of the forms and surfaces that the ceiling shelters.

More than Meets the Eye

Every builder and architect has had the traumatic experience of receiving a call from a distraught client right after the footings and foundations for a new home have been built but before there are any stud walls in place. The homeowner states emphatically that the house is too small and construction must stop. Without the differentiation of spaces provided by interior and exterior walls, the area enclosed by the foundation walls can look tiny. Although there's more than enough area there, our eyes tell us otherwise.

I had this happen to me once early in my career, before I'd become savvy to this common reaction. Construction was called to a halt for a week while I reassured my clients by comparing the size of each room in the new house with rooms they were familiar with in their existing home. Only after this were they comfortable with proceeding, and even then they were skeptical. They still felt that the kitchen, pantry, and mudroom were much too small. It wasn't until the cabinets were installed that these rooms took on their expected proportions, and my clients realized each space was in fact larger, not smaller, than they'd been anticipating. The cabinets give us something that we can relate to in comparison to the proportions of our bodies, and suddenly a space that appeared small now seems ample.

All this serves to illustrate that without differentiation, we have little to compare to our human scale, and so we see less space. It's the delineations of space and surface that allow us to perceive what's there with any accuracy.

THIRTEEN

Depth and Thickness

A wall that's thicker than the usual 4 in. to 6 in. has a greater sense of permanence. It feels more substantial, harking back to times when houses were made of stone, brick, or logs.

TODAY, MOST HOUSES ARE BUILT to save time and minimize costs. Since the 2x4 and 2x6 have become the standard framing materials, our houses are typically composed of walls of these thicknesses. But there's nothing that requires that a wall be so. In many cultures where other building materials are used, walls are often thicker. In this country we are familiar with the character of the adobe wall, which is 12 in. to 24 in. deep, depending on the dimensions of the adobe brick it's made from. The resulting quality of space is a dramatic departure from what we consider normal.

Many people feel a strong attraction to these thicker forms, seeing them as more solid and permanent. We tend to associate thickness with sturdiness, probably because of the kinds of structures we've seen successfully weather the elements over the centuries.

Though it would be wonderful to build with such materials as heavy timbers, brick, and stone today, for most of us the cost is prohibitive. But that doesn't mean we can't still create thick walls. We simply need to do it in a different way, by using more than one thickness of stud wall, perhaps with storage space between the two. If you think about the two sides of a wall as separate things, with the ability to be shaped independently of one another, suddenly there's a great liberation to how the space on either side of that wall can be formed.

A deeper wall can also become a form of sculpture. By figuratively scooping into the surface, you can create everything from art niches to library walls to deep windowsills. As you'll see in this chapter, even when the added depth is actually an illusion, the house still gains that sense of greater permanence that we long for in our homes today.

Thick Walls

A wall of greater than standard thickness gives a sense of permanence and solidity to the structure that it is a part of. Windows and doors that are set into the wall expose its depth and reveal the full power of its massiveness. The wall shown here runs through the middle of this house like a spine, dividing the main living spaces from the kitchen and entryway. Its presence is apparent on both levels, and it forms a backdrop for the many vistas through the house. There are many interior openings in the thick wall that offer connecting views from the spaces on one side of the spine to the other, revealing its depth in the process.

You can also create a thick wall by adding closets or cabinets to the interior of a wall, as shown in this master bedroom dressing area at right. The cabinets form the side walls of the window seat, and there's a soffit above both the window seat and the cabinetry, which continues the thickness of the wall all the way to the ceiling. If there were no soffit, and only a space above the cabinetry and the window, the illusion of the wall's thickness would disappear.

Deep-Set Windows

When a window is set into an exterior wall that's thicker than usual, the way the interior wall depth is shaped around the window can have a significant effect on the quality of light that enters. In the photo on p. 116, the wall surrounding the window has been beveled so that the light reflects off these surfaces, creating a frame of soft brightness. A window with straight side cuts through a thick wall gives a stronger contrast between the area surrounding the window and the adjacent wall surfaces. In the photo above, the depth was created by adding shelving to the interior surface of the exterior wall.

Library Walls

You can create a thick wall anywhere in the house by adding bookshelves, as in this hallway, which doubles as a small library space. If the shelves had nothing on them, the wall would seem much less substantial. It's the combination of the shelves and the infill of books that gives the walls such a sense of solidity. When used in this fashion, books are essentially like thick wallpaper. Not only do they tell you something about the people who live in the home, but they also have a wonderfully variegated character that adds great richness and color to the walls they occupy.

Wide Windowsills

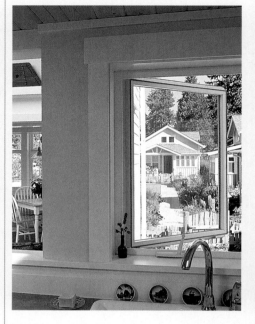

Another characteristic of a deep-set window that's appealing to many people is the resulting wide windowsill, which can be used as a plant shelf or simple exhibit space. The deeper the wall, the deeper the windowsill can be, and the larger the objects it can accommodate. Because this is such a desirable feature, some people bump out a window by a few inches to create the extra depth or thicken up the wall with an extra row of 2x4s to inexpensively obtain a wider sill.

Kitchen counter is built out from wall by 4 in. to create wider windowsill.

Wall Insets

One way to feature a piece of artwork is to indent the wall on which it is mounted. The painting in the photo above is hung at the center of a shallow indent created by adding 1-in. furring strips on top of the regular 2x4s in the areas surrounding the indented section. Wall insets can be made in other ways too, either by turning the 2x4s in a wall on their sides so that a section of wall is only 1½ in. thick, or by making a deeper inset in a thicker wall, as you'll see in the example at the end of this chapter.

Interior Sculpture

Roseville Chapel   This simple hallway in a chapel in Roseville, Minnesota, designed by Minneapolis architect Ed Kodet, beautifully illustrates the sense of permanence and solidity that a thick wall can give to a space.

Without the square deep-set windows, this would be an ordinary hallway. With them, the entire composition—the wall, the light from the hidden windows, and the luminous insets—becomes a moving interior sculpture. It's the contrast created by the glow of daylight reflecting off the surfaces of the wall insets, adjacent to the monolithic plane of the long hallway wall, that makes the effect so powerful.

A thick wall can also become a wonderfully moldable element in a home—almost like an object shaped out of clay—as can be seen here with a fireplace that's set into a freestanding wall segment (a Pod of Space) dividing a dining room from a living room in this Santa Fe residence. The fireplace is see-through, making it possible to perceive the depth of the wall from either side; and because the wall does not extend to the ceiling or to either sidewall, it appears as interior sculpture, not simply a wall between rooms.

An adobe wall that's been shaped and sculpted into an organic form, like the fireplace in the Taos home shown below, gives even more of this experience. The house is clearly made out of something much more malleable than 2x4s.

Distinctly Sculptural

THE HOUSE SHOWN HERE underwent a dramatic remodel and transformation before its new owners, a couple with grown children, moved in. They loved the site and the surrounding views, but the floor plan left a lot to be desired. Architects Karen and Bob Gould of GouldEvans of Kansas City were hired to help turn the existing house into a place that fit the couple's lifestyle and allowed for comfortable everyday living, as well as for frequent entertaining.

This remodeled Kansas City home is unusually sculptural in character, with thick walls and deep-set windows used throughout.

Daylight bounces off the wall segments perpendicular to each window surface, giving a wonderfully soft quality to the light entering the room.

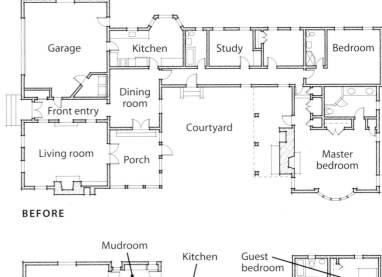

BEFORE

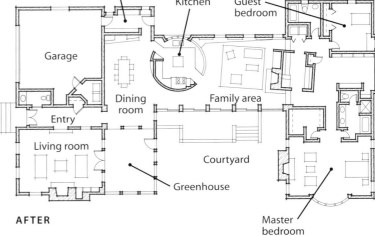

AFTER

The garage, the formal living room, and the front entry between them were left in their original positions, but the center area of the floor plan was completely changed—demolished down to the floor platform, in fact, and then enlarged and rebuilt—to accommodate dining, kitchen, and family gathering areas. Throughout this space, the architects used **thick walls** in various ways to give it a dynamic and sculptural quality. Although the character of the architecture is unusual, and may not appeal to everyone, the lessons to be learned here are many and can be applied to any style of home.

The new central living space is essentially one large rectangular room, covered by a barrel-vaulted ceiling and separated into different activity areas by the kitchen, which floats in the middle of the room as a freestanding object—a Pod of

Space (see Differentiation of Parts, Chapter 12). Thick walls are used along both sides of the room, but the one on the west side is dramatically different from the one on the east side.

If you look at the floor plan, you'll see that the mullions between the windows on the west side of the room, looking out over the central outdoor courtyard, are quite thick—2 ft. thick, in fact—and are capped by a wide floating shelf. So as you look along the wall from the dining room past the rust-colored plaster wall of the kitchen, you don't see the windows themselves at all but only the reflected daylight that bounces off the deep mullions into the room. They are, in effect, a series of **deep-set windows.** The hidden light source engages the imagination and makes you want to explore and see what's out there. It's only as you move past the kitchen and into the family sitting

The thick wall between the dining room and the mudroom provides places for exhibit and storage. The wall insets in the kitchen "pod" to the right are also suitable for displaying artwork.

instead of mirror there are windows, and the display surface is also a real windowsill. The dark wood sill extends all the way along the wall, tying the composition together, and serving as a beltline (see Differentiation of Parts) as well as display area.

Small wall insets were also created in the dining room, on the back surface of the curved kitchen wall. Notched into the plaster surface, they can be used either to exhibit artwork or simply as interesting sculptural forms in their own right.

Even in the existing, largely unchanged parts of the house, such as the formal living room, the Goulds have thickened walls to create shelves, display places, and shutter storage.

space that the views out to the courtyard and beyond are revealed. The result is much more interesting and visually stimulating than if this wall were composed of a series of windows in a wall of regular thickness. Discovering the views once you move into the space animates the whole experience of moving from one activity area to the next.

On the east side of the room, the thick wall is used to create storage space and display places for both the dining and the family areas. In the dining room, the architects created a **wall inset** between two storage cabinets and lined it with a mirror so that it functions much like a deep-set window. The wood countertop is equivalent to a **wide windowsill** and functions both as an exhibit surface and as a place to put serving dishes during formal dinners. The same technique is used in the living room (see the photo on the facing page), but here

In the more formal rooms of the house, thick walls are used to add character (and storage space).

PART TWO

Light

NO MATTER HOW MUCH CARE AND EFFORT YOU PUT INTO THE
sculpting of a home's interior, if there's no light, you won't be
aware of the shapes of the spaces that surround you. Light has the
power to reveal the forms of things, to bring definition to their
textures and colors, and in so doing to give the spaces they inhabit
a particular ambiance.

Our language is rich with phrases that indicate the importance
of this medium. We "shed light on" something that is obscure.
We are "in the dark" when we don't understand. And we are
"illuminated" by someone's insights. All of these metaphors point
out the extraordinary importance that light plays in our ability
to perceive.

Architects use light to animate their designs in ways that subtly
influence our perceptions, engaging us in the exploration of interior
space and helping to create that longed-for feeling of home.

FOURTEEN

Light to Walk Toward

Our attraction to light subliminally draws us toward the brightness at the end of a hallway or passage and makes the spaces accessed along the route more engaging as a result.

W E OFTEN HEAR that in near-death experiences people find themselves moving toward a brilliant light. But it's not just in death that we have this automatic response to light. In our everyday lives we humans have a strong built-in instinct to move toward light, which results in a significant sense of well-being.

This is such a simple principle, yet it is also one of the most powerful. As you observe the world around you, you'll notice that in many of the places you find the most engaging, this principle is at play. Conversely, many of the places that feel the most oppressive are lacking it.

If you've ever lived in a house where all the bedrooms and bathrooms are accessed from a long, poorly lit hallway, you'll know how it feels when there is no light to walk toward. The entire wing of the house feels dreary and depressing. Most people assume it's the hallway that's the problem, but that's not necessarily the case. A hallway can be quite beautiful if there is a light source at the end of it.

When designing a house from scratch, you can align a doorway with a window directly across from it, so the window will beckon you in. Relocate the window to some other area of the wall, however, and there's much less to engage you. If it's not possible to put a window across from the door, then you can use a lighted picture in its place—anything that will focus light onto the surface you are moving toward.

The same holds true for any major axis through the house. Place a window or lighted surface at the far end, and you'll be pulled toward it, and drawn to explore along the way. There's a sense of delight and enchantment about a house that artfully employs this principle.

Light at the End of the Tunnel

If you've ever walked through a dark tunnel, you may recall the experience of relief you felt at seeing the light at the far end. We can use this experiential conditioning in the design of a home to draw someone through the darker areas and toward the light place.

The house shown here is organized around a long passageway, with rooms opening off either side. Without the light source at the far end, the experience of moving from one end of the house to the other would seem dull and uninviting. Instead of attracting you toward the light source, there would be nothing but the monotony of an entirely shady walkway. The light at the end of the tunnel animates the walkway and lends vitality to the experience of living in the house. Interestingly, if the rest of the passage were more brightly lit, the effect would be less dramatic because there would be less contrast.

Window at the End of a Hallway

The easiest way to create a strong contrast between the wall surfaces that define a hallway and the light source at the far end is to use a window that lets in plenty of daylight. The window serves admirably as the light at the end of the tunnel.

In the house shown here (and on p. 100), the architects were confronted with a tricky problem. The original front entry to the house delivered guests into a long dark hallway that ran the length of the adjacent garage. In their design solution, they created a central courtyard that could be seen from a number of places in the house. By aligning a window into the courtyard with the hallway linking the front door to the living space, the entry process became far more inviting than it used to be. It leads guests and homeowners alike inward, toward the brightness of the courtyard.

Once you step through the thickened doorway that aligns with the back wall of the garage, you enter a space that, although still part of the hallway, offers a view into the

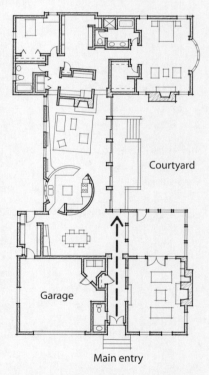

Courtyard

Garage

Main entry

main living area, which then becomes the draw that leads you farther into the home. So the window has been used to provide a subliminal lure. You automatically move toward the light and in so doing discover the rest of the house. Without the window, you might well wonder where to go.

Lighted Picture at the End of a Vista

Window at the End of a Main Axis

If it is not possible to end a hallway with a window, you can use a lighted painting or even simply a lighted wall instead. This is a wonderfully cost-effective solution to remedying the oppressiveness of a drab vista. In the photo shown here, a short hallway leads to a dressing room to the right. A recessed light above the dresser provides an attractive focus that leads you in. Just as with the windows in the previous examples, if the light and picture were removed, the view would be much less engaging and there'd be little to enliven the experience of moving toward the closet.

This technique works in any situation where you want to focus attention. For example, aligning a lighted painting with a doorway makes the process of moving into the room far more attractive—it encourages you to step inside. The wall at the far end of the U-shaped kitchen shown here is lit by a skylight above, which draws you in.

The same concept can be used where there's a strong visual axis of some kind, even though there are no walls to define a hallway. In this house, the plan is divided into two halves by an implied hallway that runs from the front to the back of the house. Though there are few walls, the beams in the ceiling define the walkway, and there are windows at either end that draw you toward them. When the windows are removed, the walkway no longer draws you in. It's as though the windows bring life to the walkway, and involve you in the process of moving through the house.

CONTRAST

CONTRAST

Light and Dark One particularly dramatic place to use the principle of Light to Walk Toward is in a dark stairway. Many staircases have no light source or window at their base, or at the place where the stairway turns, so as you descend the stairs you are moving toward a dark wall— an oppressive experience even when the stairway itself is well lit. By placing a lighted picture on the wall directly in front of the stair run, you have something to walk toward—something that uplifts rather than oppresses your spirits.

The Long View

THIS SMALL HOUSE for a young couple, designed by Jim Estes of Estes Twombly in Rhode Island, uses the principle of Light to Walk Toward in a very straightforward way to animate the movement through the house. Arriving at the front door—a pair of French doors in this case—you are welcomed by a long view through the house. At the far end of the vista is the kitchen, with one of its windows directly in line with the front door. This window is the first of six that open up the entire corner where the kitchen is located. So it is not only the window that's visible from the entry that attracts you toward it. There's a brilliant glow from the daylight reflecting off the white ceiling that tells you there's more here than meets the eye. As you proceed down the hallway and more windows are revealed, the open corner itself becomes the focal point that draws you farther into the house.

Without the alignment of the left-hand window with the front door, the long view through the house falls flat (see the smaller photo on the facing page). There's nothing attracting your attention to the far end of the space. The house seems smaller too, because the line of sight is stopped at the back wall.

Partway along the hallway, just behind the front entry closet, sits the stairway to the second floor. Here, too, a window has been used to lead you up the first two risers, at which point the

As you move inside, the kitchen windows, now revealed as a series of windows that wrap around the corner, continue to attract your attention. The entire corner becomes the bright place at the end of the vista.

PICTURE THIS

If the window is taken out at the end of the view from the front door through to the kitchen at the far wall, there's much less to draw you in and to encourage you to explore the house further.

With windows wrapped around two sides, the whole kitchen is bathed in light. By lowering the windowsills all the way to the level of the countertop, even this darker surface helps reflect daylight deep into the space and makes the kitchen a beacon to walk toward from anywhere on the main level.

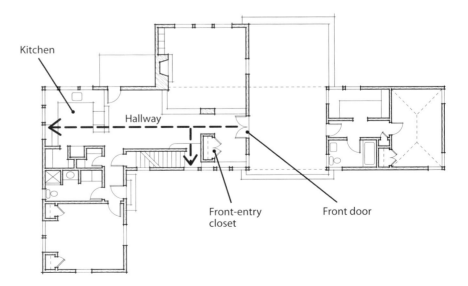

Kitchen

Hallway

Front-entry closet

Front door

stairway turns. Estes often uses this technique to make the stairs he designs attractive focal points. He'll place from two to four steps in the first run of stairs and align them with a window directly ahead. This makes the beginning of the process of changing levels a very pleasing experience. As you take the first couple of steps, you move up next to the window, the source of the light. Before learning about this principle, you might have assumed that the delight arises from the access to view that it brings. Although this is certainly part of it, the feeling of excitement is more the result of the movement toward light. Even if there were a translucent screen obscuring the view, you'd still feel exhilarated by the proximity to the light source. I imagine that the homeowners sometimes pause here for a moment before continuing up the stairs.

Exeter Library

Louis Kahn, one of the giants of twentieth-century architecture and a true genius with light, frequently used strategically placed windows to draw people from place to place in his buildings. In this view along a tall hallway at the Exeter Library (1972) in Exeter, New Hampshire, the window at the end of the hall exerts a powerful pull, encouraging visitors to explore further. You'll also see that Kahn has aligned the upper wall on the right with the window, so that it acts as a reflecting surface.

The window at the landing is located at the pivot point of the stair, one riser up from the main level. The window exerts a strong pull toward it, encouraging us to move upstairs.

FIFTEEN

Light Intensity Variation

Without variations in light intensity, the interior of a house can appear bland and monotonous, however interesting the actual shape of the space.

Have you ever noticed when you go into an inexpensive discount store everything is lit to the same level of intensity? Although there is plenty of light to see by, nothing is highlighted and nothing is downplayed. Everything looks the same. Compare that experience with a visit to a high-end department store, where there will typically be several different types of lighting. The brightest is focused on particular featured displays, while another type gives general ambient lighting, and there is some lower level lighting along the walkways. Your attention is drawn to the featured items, but you also find the less brightly lit areas more interesting because of the variation.

The same principle can be applied to house design. Whether considering where to place windows or how to position light fixtures, it's important to understand that our senses are stimulated by contrast. As with the discount store, a room that is uniformly lit appears flat and uninteresting. Many houses have surface-mounted fixtures in the center of every ceiling—the epitome of lighting monotony. Although these provide adequate lighting to see by, they're often not used because the room looks washed out with them turned on. Instead, homeowners bring in table lamps and floor-standing torchères to create a wider variety of lighting experience and to give the room some life.

The placement of windows in a house can dramatically enhance variations in light intensity. Vary the amount of window area from space to space, as well as the orientation, and the house will become far more alive and enjoyable to live in.

Layers of Light and Shade

In our culture we tend to worship light, and we rarely embrace anything other than brightness. But by so doing, we miss the full impact of the light areas because there is no shadiness to contrast with them. When a house celebrates the dark as well as the light, there's a much broader range of moods created within the spaces as a result.

In the photo shown above, if there were no bright place at the end of this Sequence of Places, the darker space containing the desk might well feel oppressive; but when the final layer is a bright one, the shady place seems more intriguing, and the bright place seems all the more attractive. It's the contrast between the two that enlivens both. Allowing a house to have at least a few areas that are shadier adds depth and intensity to the experience of living there.

Light Defines Form

You can use light and shade to help inform the eye about the shape of a surface. This is particularly useful when a surface has an unusual form. If the entire surface is uniformly lit, it is much more difficult to perceive its shape. Look at this curved ceiling with ribs every 6 ft. It is supported by thick wall sections between each of the sliding doors that run the length of the room. We can understand the shape of the ceiling and the shape of the thick wall sections because of the light variations.

At the lower edges of the curved ceiling, there's a darkly shaded area created by the horizontal lintel that runs along the wall. Tucked in behind this lintel and between each of the ceiling ribs is a bright pin spot light whose beam spreads wider the farther from the room edge it goes. So the eye sees not only the light but also the shape that the light makes. We are given the visual information to see the curvature. But if the entire room were lit more brightly, there would be little to help us understand the ceiling shape.

Indented Windows

Brilliance in a Dark Place

One of the great attractions of deep-set indented windows and wide windowsills is the variation in light intensity between the thick wall that's perpendicular to the window surface and the adjacent wall surface that faces into the room. The thick wall is bright because it is reflecting the light from the window, while the wall surface that faces into the room is considerably darker since it's reflecting much less light. The contrast in brightness has an alluring beauty to it. In the photo shown here, the thick wall is beveled so the effect is not quite as intense, but you can still see the difference between the bright beveled surface and the darker surrounding wall. The beveled area is almost like a picture frame that focuses attention on the window.

The logical extreme of this principle is the introduction of a bright light source into a place that is otherwise very dark. This technique is used in the theater to rivet your attention on the actor in the spotlight. All other sensory information is shrouded in shadow. The only thing to look at is where the light falls.

I first became aware of this phenomenon when visiting a number of chapels and religious buildings designed by Swiss-French architect Le Corbusier (1887–1965), who is a master at using light to affect the senses. In a chapel at La Tourette, a monastery built in Eveux, France, in 1953, the architect introduced a shaft of light above the altar, effecting in the onlooker a deep sense of the mystery of life. Even for someone without any interest in the spirit, the experience of being in such a place evokes an awareness of the extraordinary power and majesty of light—the revealer of all form.

Color Defines Form   In a room that's fairly uniformly lit, color can be used to define the form of a curved ceiling. Here, the adjacent wall is painted a dark color to highlight the ceiling shape. If the wall were painted white like the ceiling, the ceiling form would be much less clear.

137

Southwest Light

Floor and ceiling surfaces adjacent to the few south-facing windows are points of brilliance along a shaded hallway.

THE LIGHT IN NEW MEXICO is intense. Because it is so far south, the altitude so high, and the vegetation so sparse given the dryness of the climate, there is little protection from the sun's brilliance. As a result, residential architects and designers must contend with some difficult challenges. The sun's direct rays can cause interior heat buildup, significant bleaching of furnishings, and even eye strain. To avoid overwhelming a space with daylight, window size and orientation are critical things to consider in the design process. It is important to control the amount of direct sunlight entering a house. Unlike a home built in a more northerly location, where sunlight is welcomed most of the year, in New Mexico it's best to minimize the windows looking to the west and east, and glass that faces south can be a problem even in the winter months when the angle of the sun is low.

This home, designed by architect Robyn Gray for a retired couple, beautifully illustrates the dramatic quality of space that results when daylight and windows are introduced sparingly along the face of the house that receives direct light. A primary feature of this home is its long walkway, which connects the living spaces and the two bedroom wings and runs the full length of the house.

Because it is located on the south side, where windows have been kept to a reasonable minimum, there's a wonderful interplay of **light and shade.** As you look along the length of the walkway, you'll see that at the two places where there are windows, there's a brilliant glow to the surrounding surfaces, while adjacent spaces languish in the shadows. Even though the windows are not large, the light is intense. It's the resulting contrast that gives a dynamic quality to the entire house. The bright areas draw you toward them as you move along the walkway, whereas the darker areas impart a deep sense of calm. If the entire hallway were flooded with direct sunlight, the experience would be overwhelming.

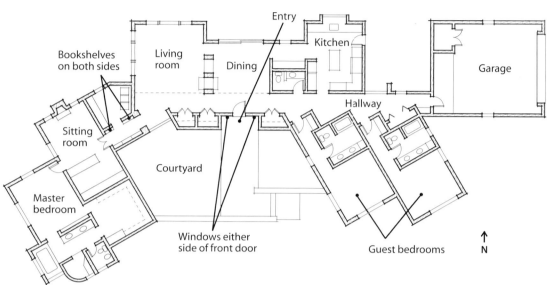

The patterns of light and shadow cast by the windows are a wonderful example of the engaging quality that Light Intensity Variation can give to a space.

Pools of light on the living room floor exert a strong attraction, drawing us into the bright space from the more subdued and shady library hallway.

In fact, if you look closely, you'll see that Gray has placed the south-facing windows in such a way that they lead you to investigate the home's primary living spaces, with one window opening into the living room and another pair, either side of the front door, opening into the dining room. Remembering back to Chapter 14, you'll recall that a bright light at the end of a hallway draws you toward it. Here a similar principle is used, but in this case the brilliant pools of light are not at the ends of the hallway. Instead, the white ceiling acts as a reflector, and the spaces on either side are in shadow. It's an automatic reflex to move toward the place that's bathed in light.

A little farther down the walkway, Gray used a similar technique to focus attention on the doorways to the two guest bedrooms. Small skylights bring daylight into the hallway and, just like a light fixture at a front door, indicate that this is a point of entrance.

She used skylights in other places as well, such as the powder room, to create an attractive focal point as well as to give the room a certain mysteriousness. By hiding the light source but letting the

In this skylit powder room, the light bounces off the wall and past the deep beams of the ceiling, giving the room a very peaceful and inspirational feel. It is an example of what happens when you introduce "brilliance in a dark place."

In the hallway along the bedroom wing, pools of light from small skylights above each doorway and each set of bookshelves continue the theme of Light Intensity Variation seen in the more public parts of the house.

sunlight bounce off the wall and down into the room below, she brought all the surfaces into sharp relief. The surfaces that receive direct light, like the top of the partition wall between the toilet and the sink and the sides of the beams in the ceilings, appear very bright, while those that are in shadow, like the side walls of the toilet partition and the bottoms of the beams, are dark and hidden. But in combination the shapes of both the partition wall and the beams are highly defined. If there were a bright light on in the room itself, much of this definition would disappear, and the room, although still attractive, would be far less intriguing.

Similarly, the contrast between the bright places and the darker areas along the walkway gives the forms of the walkway and the fireplace mass much sharper definition. Notice what happens when the walkway is uniformly in shade (photo below right). With no brightness to define the edge of the fireplace or the ceiling edge of the walkway, it is difficult to distinguish the shape of the space. It is actually hard to tell that there is a walkway there at all.

The Pantheon

When you visit a building like the Pantheon in Rome (built 118–126), you experience firsthand the transcendent quality that a brilliant source of light can create. As the sun moves across the sky each day, the ellipse of light cast by the center oculus traces its way across the wall surfaces below, revealing each of its features for only a few minutes before returning them to darkness for another day.

With the reflected light from the doorway removed, you can't even tell there's a hallway here. Everything is suddenly drab and homogeneous.

SIXTEEN

Reflecting Surfaces

*By understanding how to situate windows and light fixtures in relation
to walls and ceilings you can make a house much brighter and cheerier
than it would otherwise be.*

MOST PEOPLE ARE DEEPLY AFFECTED by the amount and quality of light that permeates their living and working environments. When a space is filled with light, and especially with daylight, we tend to feel happier and more balanced, while too little light on a regular basis can make us feel tired and irritable—even depressed. By using the wall and ceiling surfaces in the house in combination with the windows and light fixtures that are required for each room, it's possible to dramatically increase the amount of light available without adding to the cost. It's simply a matter of knowing how to place them.

When positioning a window or skylight, the key is to place it as close to the wall or ceiling (or both) as possible so that the adjacent perpendicular surface gets bathed in daylight, which is then reflected deep into the room. When positioning a light fixture to maximize this effect, the approach depends on the type of fixture involved. The goal is to get the cone of light from the bulb to wash the reflecting wall or ceiling surface with light, which then, as with the window, gets bounced further into the space. The lighter the color of the wall or ceiling, the better these strategies work. A dark color will absorb most of the light that strikes it, so although the wall itself may look beautiful, it won't reflect much and so won't have much impact on the brightness of the rest of the room.

I've had many clients over the years report that they feel much more alert and energized after moving into new homes that employ these techniques, and they've each cited the increased access to daylight as being a major reason for the change.

Wall Washing

Reflective Ceiling

When a window or skylight is located directly adjacent to a perpendicular wall, it's as though both the glass area and the wall surface become part of a large light fixture during the daytime. The wall reflects the available daylight into the space and increases the brightness of the room. In this stairway, the windows have only a narrow strip of wood trim between them and the adjacent walls on both sides of the stair landing, and there is substantially more light bounced into the entire stairway as a result. If the goal is to maximize the brightness of the space, the lighter the color of the wall, the better this technique will work.

Sometimes, however, the architect's objective is to create a certain mood with a soft light source. In such cases, it may be desirable to use a darker wall color. This will bounce less light into the space, but will give the room a warm glow instead. In the photo on p.142, the edge of the skylight has been aligned perfectly with the wood-sheathed wall beneath it, giving a soft pinkish-colored cast to the light.

When the top edge of a window is located tight up against the ceiling, the entire surface becomes a reflector. Because the light received by the ceiling is usually reflected from the surrounding exterior ground surfaces, the lighter the color of the ground outside, the brighter the ceiling will be.

I designed a house several ago that was very close to a lake, with nothing obstructing the view. As the sun set each evening, the rays from the waning sun would strike the water surface and bounce from there into the dining room and living room. Since the dining room windows extended all the way to the ceiling, the patterns of the

water's movement were reflected on the ceiling, creating the most incredible patterns. I can't claim to have planned this feature, but it was easily the most celebrated aspect of the house for its residents.

The same effect can be created with bright uplighting wall sconces. The kitchen shown above has excellent ambient lighting supplied by a series of halogen wall sconces that throw their light onto the white barrel-vaulted ceiling. The entire ceiling surface becomes a brilliant reflector that lights the entire room.

Hidden Light Source

A powerful experience can be created by hiding the daylight source completely and allowing only the reflected light to be seen. You can do this by placing a skylight at the top of a shaft that extends down to the ceiling plane of the interior space, as shown here. The brilliance of the reflecting surface has an almost magical quality because you can't immediately see what is lighting it. This technique has been used in many famous religious buildings of the past to increase the sense of mystery and wonder. In a way, the light is being used metaphorically to suggest the relationship between man and spirit. We experience the radiance, but cannot directly see the source.

Light Coves

Another way to use the ceiling surface as a reflector is to light it from a cove on the wall below. This can be done on one side of the room only or all around the space. As you can see from the examples shown here, the lighting hidden by the coves gives a warm glow to the ceiling. Light coves are particularly attractive in the evening hours, when other lighting levels are lower. I have used this technique a lot in my own work and will sometimes design the cove to double as exhibit space, such as a plate rail.

One important detail to be aware of when designing a light cove using small bright lights is to not place the bulbs too close to either the wall or the ceiling surface. If you do, each bulb will create a hot spot, which often ends up looking like a mistake. By keeping the bulbs at least 4 in. away from the adjacent reflecting surface and by using a flat paint without sheen to it, you can minimize this problem.

Doubling the Space

To this point, we have only spoken about reflecting light off a blank surface, but a mirror will, of course, reflect both the view and the light. This characteristic can be used in all sorts of innovative ways that will not only brighten a room but also make it appear to be significantly larger than it is. You may have seen this technique used in restaurants, where it appears as if there were another room of tables and guests adjacent to the one you are in.

Bathrooms are ideal places to make the most of this application. By extending the mirror surface all the way over to the side walls, to the countertop or backsplash, and to the ceiling above, you can make the room appear double the size and give it a sleekly tailored look at the same time. With no frame around the mirror, the eye can easily believe that there is a continuation of the space on the other side of the wall. And although in this situation we know full well this is not so, most of us find this a pleasing illusion.

The Color of Reflection   The house shown here beautifully illustrates the difference that ceiling color makes on reflectivity and on the resulting feel of the space beneath. Both of these images are of rooms with similar configurations and with a band of clerestory windows hugging the ceiling plane. The ceiling at left is covered with a dark wood paneling, whereas the ceiling at right is made of drywall, painted white. You can clearly see that though there is still some light bouncing off the dark wood ceiling most is absorbed, and the surface appears heavier and lower as a result. The drywall ceiling, however, is bright and highly reflective, and the ceiling seems almost ethereal.

If you were to stand in each space, your senses would be convinced that the room with the darker ceiling is shorter, even though they are in fact the same height. Neither solution is right or wrong obviously. They simply have different effects on the spaces they shelter, and when reflected light is needed to make a room brighter, a lighter color is critical.

Alive with Light

W<small>E LOOKED CLOSELY</small> at this Minnesota home in Chapter 4, Ceiling Height Variety. As you look at the photos shown here, you'll see that Architect Mark Kawell used both walls and ceilings throughout the house as reflecting surfaces to bring definition to the shapes of the spaces he crafted with changes in ceiling height. In combination, these two principles create an animated and sculpted interior that comes alive with light. Let's look at how Kawell accomplished this.

Wherever there is a window, reflecting surfaces are close at hand to bounce the light they receive farther into the space and to focus attention on the forms that are the most brightly lit. At either end of the cathedral-ceilinged main living area, for example, there's a large triangular window that mimics the form of the ceiling above (see the top photo on p. 148). Because of the window's proximity to the ceiling surface, it becomes a reflector, bouncing daylight into the kitchen area at one end and into the living room at the other. In addition, since these ceiling areas are brighter than all the other surfaces in the space, they are visual focal points, and their shapes are clearly defined by the gradation of light intensity. The area closest to the window is the brightest,

Cove lighting is used along many of the floating shelves, so that by day or by night the broad expanses of vaulted ceiling are bathed in light, giving the whole house a warm glow.

As well as using Ceiling Height Variation in an innovative way, this Minnesota home employs these same ceiling surfaces as huge reflectors to bounce daylight deep into the interior.

becoming softer and less intense as the distance from the window increases. This helps our eyes to understand the shape of the surface.

In other places in the house, the tops of windows meet the ceiling surface, with no separating wall surface between. At both corners of the living room the windows extend to the linear floating shelf that runs the length of the room. While most of the undersurface of this shelf is in shadow, at these corner windows it is bathed in light. This again creates a point of focus for the eye, drawing your attention to the surrounding vegetation, and extending your perception of space beyond the boundaries of the house walls.

In addition to the bounced light from windows, Kawell uses the same ceiling surfaces to reflect the light from **cove lighting** throughout the house. The floating shelves do more than simply vary the ceiling height. They also conceal continuous cove lighting that gives every vaulted room a warm glow. This is apparent during the day, but at night it is a dramatic feature of the design, transforming the experience of the space and creating different focal points. During the daylight hours the two ends of the main living space are the focal points, but at night the center of the space, where the axes of the two vaulted ceilings intersect, becomes the focus. The entire vaulted ceiling surface glows, and because the lighting strip is at the lowest point of the vault, it looks a little like a sky at sunrise or sunset, when the sun is just below the horizon. Although you might not consciously make this association if you were sitting in the space, the effect can evoke a powerful sense of calm and well-being, just as a sunrise or sunset does.

In the corner of the living room, the top of the windows align with the adjacent ceiling plane, turning the entire surface into a reflector.

And, finally, Kawell also uses the underside of the shelf, as well as the perpendicular walls below, to reflect light from wall sconces at key locations, such as the piano alcove and the built-in buffet. In addition to a recessed light directly above the piano keyboard, there is also a bright spot on the ceiling to either side of the piano. These are produced by the wall sconces and give added brightness to the entire area. The recessed light provides the task lighting for reading music or seeing the piano keys, but the wall sconces provide the warm glow and create the ambiance. One type of light is practical, the other aesthetic, but both are required for the making of a rich experience in which to listen to music.

Walls are used as reflectors too. In this view from the sunroom through to the piano alcove, a pair of wall sconces illuminate the dining room's built-in buffet.

Wall sconces in the piano alcove to the right of the kitchen bounce light off the surrounding wall surfaces as well as off the floating shelf above.

SEVENTEEN

Window Positioning

*Windows can be no more than openings in the wall to let in light
and air, or they can be beautiful and powerful connectors between the
inner and outer worlds.*

I N MOST HOUSES, windows are positioned with only minimal consideration given to how they introduce light into interior spaces and with surprisingly little regard for potential exterior views. Typically, they are
placed symmetrically on either side of the centerline of the room or in the
middle of the wall. But there's so much more that a window, or set of windows, can do for a space and for the house as a whole. From the exterior, the
arrangement of windows can give the home much of its personality as well as
a sense of integrity, while from the interior, each window can be placed to
maximize the amount of light and view for the space it opens into.

All too often a house plan is selected based on interior requirements and
the appearance of the front facade. Only occasionally are alterations made to
tailor the plan so that windows are positioned to take advantage of the special
features of the site. This is why you'll often see new homes that turn their
backs on magnificent views or that have large expanses of glass facing north
and tiny slit windows facing south—exactly the reverse of what you'd want
for energy efficiency in northern climates.

When you work with an architect, orientation to the sun, special views,
and other major site features are documented in the beginning of the
design process. This ensures that the resulting house takes full advantage
of the assets of the site. There's a dramatic difference between a house
designed using this approach and one that makes
do with a plan that wasn't designed for or tailored
to the land it's built on. When the site is considered from the start, land
and house become one,
the windows providing
the connecting mem-
brane between the two.

Daylight Fixture

When a window is placed adjacent to the side wall of a room or is abutted tight to the ceiling, the entire wall or ceiling surface reflects the available daylight into the space, making it appear bright and cheery. The window in combination with the wall and/or ceiling essentially turns into a light fixture for the room—but not one you can purchase from a store, attach to the wall, and turn on and off with a switch. Here, the light source is the sun, and the surfaces perpendicular to the window are the reflectors within the fixture. So we can think of the entire composition as a Daylight Fixture.

If the same window were placed in the center of the wall, without the surrounding perpendicular surfaces to reflect the daylight, the room would be significantly darker. The wall area surrounding the window would also be significantly darker. There's nothing inherently wrong with setting a window in the center of the wall like this, but it is valuable to know that placement can dramatically affect the brightness of the room in which the window is located.

Centered on the Middle

Sometimes you may want to draw attention to a particular view or axis through the house. An excellent way to do this is to place a window or series of windows so that they line up with the center of the doorway into the space. By combining the attractive force of light, as we saw in Light to Walk Toward, with the power of aligning one thing with another, as we'll see in Alignments, you create a visual axis that is impossible to miss. Together they rivet your attention and provide a focus as you enter the room. You can almost feel your spine straighten as you look at the photo above.

You can also bring focus to a room by organizing the windows into a centered composition. We'll discuss this concept further in Composition, but it's important to note here that a center window or group of windows adds importance to the room and brings those using the space to attention, at least on a subliminal level.

Windowsill Height

The relative comfort of a room can be dramatically affected by the height of the windows off the floor. There's nothing more frustrating than sitting down at an informal eating area, for example, and finding that the windowsill is located just high enough that it obstructs the view to the garden beyond. It creates the same sense of irritation as when you are driving across a river and the guard rail on either side of the bridge completely blocks the view.

My rule of thumb is to make the windowsill no more than 2 ft. 4 in. off the floor for living areas and bedrooms where there is a significant view beyond. At this height, you can easily see out when sitting on a chair.

When locating a window above a countertop or desktop I like to bring the windowsill all the way down to the height of the horizontal work surface. This gives maximum connection to the views and minimizes the awareness of the membrane between inside and out. Even when the view is not particularly attractive, keeping the sill within 4 in. to 6 in. of the countertop tends to make the room feel more open and airy.

Window Whimsy

Light from Above

Windows can be used in all manner of ways to add character to a room. When you use them in a playful way, there are no rules, though it's easy to overdo whimsy, so unless you are really sure of what you are doing, use some restraint. With whimsy, less is usually more. Here, architect Frank Karreman used a series of small square windows at the stairway. Not only do they add three peek-a-boo spots for his children to enjoy as they go up and down stairs, but they also add an unusual flair to a traditional bungalow exterior.

A very different experience can be created when the windows in a room are located high in the space or even in the roof itself. When skylights are used to light a room, and the ceiling surface is used as part of the "daylight fixture," the room is flooded with light. Although in warmer climates skylights can be a problem—because direct sunlight produces a lot of unwanted heat—in more moderate climes the effect is both beautiful and uplifting-—similar in fact to the way you might feel outside on a bright day. In locations with many overcast days, this technique can be especially beneficial; the

reflected light from the walls and ceiling give the impression of brightness even when outdoor light levels are low.

Clerestory windows can produce a different, though equally dramatic effect. When such windows are placed adjacent to the ceiling surface, it gives the impression that the ceiling is floating. Because of the brightness of the daylight entering through the line of windows, the eye is fooled into believing that there's nothing much supporting the ceiling and it appears to defy gravity.

ILLUSION

Corner Windows There are some tricks that architects use to make a space seem larger than it really is. One of the favorite techniques is to make the corner of a room transparent by replacing the usual structure with windows. Where the eye expects structure, instead there is glass and view. And because the corner usually defines the boundary of the room in question, there is also the sense of expansiveness since one's vision is not restricted in the usual way. When combined with Diagonal Views (see Chapter 5), the effect is particularly dramatic.

Surrounded by Windows

L ANE WILLIAMS, the architect for this simple ranch house remodel in Washington State, made modifications to the window configurations throughout the house and relocated the kitchen to transform it into a place of beauty and warmth. The views to the north, toward the ocean, were already spectacular. But the windows in the original house, built in the early 1970s, did little to enhance them. As with most ranch houses, the old windows were standard casements ("crank-outs") surrounded by basic moldings. Because the views were north facing, and no thought had been given to light from other directions, the house seemed subdued and a little gloomy as there was never any direct sunlight in the main living spaces. What Williams accomplished with the redesign was to position the new set of windows to more elegantly frame the views on the north side. And he introduced

some major living spaces on the south side of the house, to provide access for south light.

In place of the original double pair of casements in the master bedroom, for example, Williams added a gracious sitting bay surrounded by windows. Even the corners of the bay are opened to the view, so there's the sense that the entire window seat extends into the landscape. The resulting connection within the room to the surrounding views is pronounced. Had the window area been made smaller and the corner windows removed, there'd be far less connection established. The windowsill is only a few inches above the height of the cushion, which means that the ocean view is visible from the bed. Had the sill been higher, the view would have disappeared.

PICTURE THIS

The new bedroom window bay in this remodeled ranch house is made almost entirely of windows. Remove the corner windows and it feels like a much more interior space with much less connection to the surroundings and the ocean beyond.

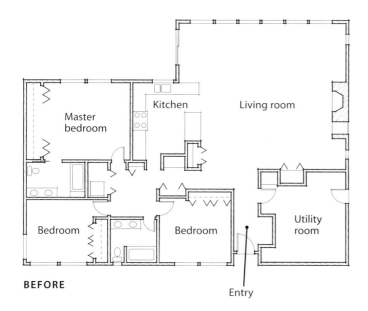

BEFORE

Master bedroom

Kitchen

Living room

Bedroom

Bedroom

Utility room

Entry

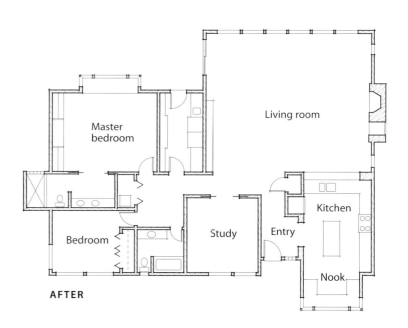

AFTER

Master bedroom

Living room

Bedroom

Study

Entry

Kitchen

Nook

The room would still be light filled and dramatic as you walked through the space, but the most exceptional feature of the site would have been hidden from view when the owners were in bed.

Williams used a similar technique in the new kitchen (see the photo on p. 150). The old kitchen had a narrow access to the ocean view, but there was no place for an informal eating area. So the decision was made to move the kitchen to the south side of the house and to include a bay to accommodate an informal eating area. By opening the wall between the living room and the kitchen, southern light can also be seen from the living room. The walls in the eating bay serve as reflecting surfaces to bounce more daylight into the room. The window configuration is identical to the one in the master bedroom, except that here there's also a row of transom windows above, allowing more of the view of the surrounding trees to enter. The pattern of the lower windows is reflected in the upper ones, creating a beautiful composition both inside and out. On the exterior, the window frames were painted a different color to draw attention to the design. This is a good example of how color can be used to accentuate the Differentiation of Parts.

The simple geometry of the window pattern and the sense of openness amid containment, in combination with the reflecting wall and the direct sunlight bathing the sitting area, give the nook a warm glow that's highly seductive. I can easily imagine sitting here each morning, soaking up the sunshine with a cup of coffee and feeling that all is right with the world. You can get a taste from this photo of the sense of well-being that can arise from a beautifully designed and crafted space.

The living room is by far the largest room in the house, and with its wide expanse of glass it provides little obstruction to the view. But without a well-composed grouping of windows even a

With a wide connecting view between living room and kitchen, the sunny feeling of the eating alcove lends warmth to the space.

The bumped-out eating alcove acts as a "daylight fixture," drawing light in as well as providing shelter for family meals.

Framed with continuous wood trim, the wall of windows in the living room is designed as the thinnest of membranes between inside and out, allowing the spectacular view to come right into the room.

great view like this would become much less dramatic. If each window were treated as a separate object, with its own casing, the composition would lose its cohesion and end up looking awkward. One's eye would tend to stop at the wall, rather than looking through it to the view beyond.

Williams decided to provide cross-ventilation for the room with windows on the east and west walls, so none of the windows on the north face needed to be openable. This allowed each pane to be larger than if it were an opening casement, and of course there is also no need for a screen, which can be an impediment to the clarity of the view.

Taken all together, the house has transcended its ranch-style roots and become an exceptional home that takes full advantage of its extraordinary site. Just because a house is bland in its original design doesn't mean that it can't easily be

upgraded to a place of style and substance. It simply needs the touch of someone who knows and understands light and composition to tweak it here and there to bring out its best features and to capitalize on the natural assets of the site.

From the outside, the home's simple ranch-house roots are clearly evident.

EIGHTEEN

Visual Weight

*Color and texture, or the combination of the two, can be used
to give a wall or ceiling increased visibility and a quality
of heft or weight.*

W HEN SPEAKING ABOUT VISUAL WEIGHT, we need to talk about color, but not in the conventional way. Color preferences vary enormously from person to person and are beyond the scope of this book. But the relative density of color used can have a powerful effect on our experience of space, and it's this characteristic that we'll discuss here.

A dark-colored surface absorbs more light than it reflects. It seems heavy in our peripheral vision, and our senses tell us that the surface must be closer to us than it actually is. It's literally as though light colors connote expansion, while dark colors connote contraction. With our present-day language preferences for bigger, lighter, and airier, we might assume that a surface that is closer and darker would automatically feel oppressive and so be undesirable, but in many cases the opposite is true. The words themselves may have negative connotations, but the quality of space created is often warm and comfortable. As we've discussed before, it's the contrast between light and dark areas that creates interest through differentiation.

Texture, too, can give a surface increased visual weight. A textured surface breaks up the light that strikes it, creating patterns of shade and shadow, which make the surface appear darker than if the entire area were smooth. For example, a ceiling with exposed joists or rafters looks darker and lower than one that is flat because the light that strikes it gets broken up.

It may seem counter-intuitive to want to make a ceiling feel lower or a wall feel closer, but sometimes this is exactly what's needed to make a room seem appro-priately proportioned, as well as to add personality.

Colored Wall

Dark-Colored Ceiling

When a wall is painted a darker color than the surrounding walls, it takes on greater importance. The eye is attracted to it and perceives it as having a kind of Visual Weight. The ambiance of the space defined by the wall will be colored by the particular color used. So this piano alcove, with its dark maroon wall, feels like the heart of the house, because this color connotes both warmth and depth. Had the wall been painted dark blue, the space would have felt cool and tranquil, almost like a still pool. If it were a bright orange, it would have taken on a more vibrant character.

A ceiling that is either sheathed with wood or painted a darker color than the walls takes on Visual Weight. In other words it seems heavier than it would if it were light in color. This is an excellent strategy to employ if a room feels too tall. Simply painting the ceiling will make it seem lower than it really is and will give the activity area it covers a greater sense of shelter and protection. Any space in which it's desirable to increase the sense of intimacy will benefit from a darker colored ceiling. The warmer the color, the more the quality of intimacy will be enhanced.

Textured Wall or Ceiling

When a wall or ceiling is highly textured, the texture will create a pattern of light and shade as either daylight or light from a wall or ceiling fixture strikes it. It will thus have much the same effect as if the entire surface had been painted a darker color.

One of the most commonly seen applications of this idea occurs in a room with exposed joists or rafters. In the home shown here, the architect used a dark-colored wood for the ceiling and exposed the rough-hewn beams to the space below, to make the room seem far more intimate than it would have if the ceiling had been the same color as the walls. You can see in this photo that the bottom surfaces of the beams appear lighter than the sides that face away from the window. This is because the bottom surfaces are actually reflecting some of the light from the windows, while the back sides of the beams receive very little light, and so reflect almost none.

Subtle Color Difference

Although architects typically use the term Visual Weight to indicate a strong contrast in color between one surface and another, the same principle applies when much subtler colors are used. As long as the eye can pick up a difference between two colors applied to adjacent surfaces, the darker of the two will have a Visual Weight that in turn accentuates the lighter colored sur-

face. You can see this clearly in the example shown above. The wall surface is painted a soft gray, which makes the white of the trim around the doors and windows seem to pop out and focus the attention. When both wall and trim are painted the same color, there's no differentiation, no difference in visual weight between the two elements, and a lot of the character of the room is lost.

Colored Alcove

A powerful application of the principle of Visual Weight is to paint an entire alcove a deeper, richer color than the rest of the room it opens onto. In a simple example of this concept, the bedroom shown here was remodeled to provide an alcove for the bed. By lowering the ceiling slightly, framing the opening with wood trim, and painting the entire alcove (including the ceiling) a deep color, the space takes on the feeling of the intimate heart of the house.

Lipstick

We discussed the effects of headbands and beltlines in Chapter 13, Differentiation of Parts. When either one is painted a distinctly different color from the surrounding surfaces, I like to think of the color as akin to lipstick. It draws attention to a tiny area, which takes on disproportionate Visual Weight because of the intensity of the color. In fact, in the photo shown here there are two different applications of Visual Weight.

First, there is the lipstick of the beltline and window trim, and, second, there is the difference in depth of color between the shingles above the beltline and the lap siding below. If both the area above and below the beltline were the same color, there'd be no difference in Visual Weight between the two and the house would seem significantly less rooted to its site.

Color It Bold

THIS LITTLE CONDO remodel is a wonderful example of the huge effect that the bold use of color can have on the look and feel of a space. When Christina and Mike Mannion bought the place there was a large staircase in the middle of the 19-ft.-high living room—a previous owner's attempt to make use of the tall central space. But the local building inspector had deemed it a fire hazard, which had scared off many potential buyers. Christina had recently graduated from architecture school and was eager to try out her new skills on a challenging

The most dramatic alteration in this condo remodel was also the least expensive—the intense color applied to the wall behind the new catwalk and staircase to the existing loft.

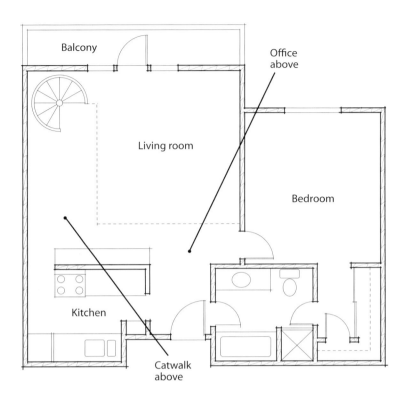

project such as this, so, instead of scaring them away, the awkward stair and odd room arrangement actually attracted them to the property and allowed them to move into an interesting new urban community at a price they could afford. Christina decided to keep the loft that extended over the kitchen, but to access this space she added a catwalk with a spiral staircase at the end, which took up significantly less floor area than the previous staircase had done.

In the original condo design, the entire living area had been 19 ft. tall, and because the associated floor area was relatively small and was centered on the doorway with arched window above, it accommodated only one activity place—the main sitting area. With the addition of the catwalk, the room has two distinctly separate places: the lowered ceilinged area beneath the catwalk, which serves as the Mannion's dining area, and the rest of the room, which is the main living space.

PICTURE THIS

If the back wall were painted white like everything else in the space, the room would be much less interesting and the activity places would be less well defined. The dining area below the catwalk feels more rooted because of the Visual Weight provided by the colored wall.

The boldly colored wall gives the right side of the room a sense of heft and presence. Wherever you are in the condominium, this wall is the dominant force.

Because the catwalk makes the left side of the space distinctly different from the right side, the space no longer feels symmetrical, and the seating can be placed off center without looking "odd."

The solution was very economical, and if Christina had done no more than this, she would have been pleased with the results. But she wanted something unique, something that would make a bit of a statement. So she decided to paint the wall above and below the catwalk a deep royal blue, which has a dramatic impact. The Visual Weight of the wall gives the space a sense of depth and solidity that it would lack if the wall were white, like all the other surfaces. The bright white of the catwalk sidewall cutting across the blue background, combined with the black of the spiral staircase, creates a wonderfully dynamic interplay of contrasts that is quite stimulating to the eye.

With a white back wall, the room seems starker and taller. In this instance, the added sense of height is not desirable, since the ceiling is already a bit too high in proportion to the width and length of the space. With the wall painted blue, the depth of color makes that side of the room feel heavier—of more substance—and draws the eye to it, no matter where you are in the room. And even though the color is applied consistently across the surface, it definitely gives the living area more character without being either difficult or expensive to install. That's a lot of bang for the buck.

NINETEEN

View and Nonview

A window doesn't have to let in the view if you don't want it to.
It can simply bring in light if the view is undesirable.

A FEW YEARS AGO I was working with a client on a kitchen remodel. She really wanted more daylight in the room but thought that she couldn't have it because the only available wall abutted a flat-roofed garage. A new window would look out directly over the black roof membrane surface of the garage, a view she couldn't live with. So she'd hired me to help her improve the interior lighting instead. But once I'd found out the problem she had with an added window, I suggested that we revisit this option before throwing it out as impossible. What if we were to use a window that allowed in light but not view? We ended up with a new art glass window that flooded the kitchen with light and also served as a beautiful work of art. The art glass selected was clear in color but patterned, so that it still let in all the available daylight. But because it obscured the view to the roof it was now a major asset to the room rather than an eyesore.

This was clearly not a complicated solution, but it didn't occur to the homeowner because it was beyond the conventional understanding of what a window is. We are often unaware of how much our preconceptions restrict the way we use building elements.

In Japanese architecture, light screens of various types are often used to allow views to be there when they are wanted and closed off when not desired. Although we don't use this strategy a lot in our own culture, we can learn by observing how this rethinking of building elements— in this case windows and window coverings— can offer all sorts of different interior experiences as a result. Just because something is always done a certain way does not mean there aren't other options.

Light but Not View

There are many places where it is desirable to let in the available daylight without also letting in the view. In the case of the house I designed for the inner ring suburb setting described and illustrated in the Introduction to this book, a neighbor's house was too close for comfort to have a regular window at the entry to the stairway.

But as we wanted to use the principle of Light to Walk Toward to draw attention to the stairway entrance, we knew that we still needed some sort of window. So we engaged an art-glass designer to create a simple design that could be used to obscure the view (see photo below).

A less expensive approach that accomplishes the same effect is to use etched glass, which gives the entering daylight a similar character to light passing through white tissue paper. In the example shown above, the neighbors across the street had a direct view into this apartment's main living space. Instead of living with constantly closed window coverings, the owners chose to have the three large panels of glass acid-etched. In this way, the panels allow in almost as much daylight as if the glass had been clear while still maintaining privacy.

One-Way View

In other situations you may want to limit the view into the house but still see out. This is a common desire at a front entry, where you may want to flood the foyer with daylight and see who is at the front door, but you don't want visitors to be able to see in easily.

In these locations you can either use a complex art glass window or a material like glass block, which obscures the view but still allows the eye to perceive the general form of what is located on the other side.

You can also use different clarities of glass block in the same location, as in the shower stall shown above. The architect combined obscuring glass block below shoulder level with clear glass block above. This way there's ample access to view and light, but limited view from the exterior. An inexpensive version of the same idea is the cafe curtain, shown here.

Art-Glass Focus

Art glass can make a wonderful focal point for a room, whether or not it is used to obscure the view beyond. When installed on a south, east, or west wall, direct sunlight creates delightful patterns that move slowly across the interior surfaces of the room with the movement of the sun. If a piece or two of beveled glass is used in the design, there will also be tiny spectrums of light at certain sun angles that add a spark of magic.

You can also use art glass on the interior of a house to make light-translucent screens between rooms, as shown here. The daylight from the windows in the library still penetrates into the living space, but the art glass panels provide a clear separation between the two areas (see also Chapter 6, Layering).

Small Panes

Sometimes, instead of using a large single panel of glass, it is desirable to frame a view in a more complex way by adding a grille or pattern to the glass. (For more about this strategy, see Chapter 20, Pattern and Geometry.) By overlaying the view with a grid that divides the glass area into segments, the view is broken into smaller, bite-sized pieces, and there is also a greater sense of enclosure from within the room.

You can accomplish the same thing with more complicated patterns as well. Several window manufacturers give buyers the option of including a special design of muntins into their standard windows—for a price, of course! This strategy does not obscure the view, but it definitely alters the way it is perceived and provides an intermediate Point of Focus at the outside surface of the home.

Through a Lens

THE POOL HOUSE featured here was designed for a beautiful turn-of-the-century home in the Berkeley Hills. The owners are big fans of Arts and Crafts style architecture and, in particular, the work of the Scottish architect Charles Rennie Mackintosh, and they wanted their new pool house to echo some of details that were typical of these two styles. Architect Hiroshi Morimoto rose to the task and provided them with a wonderful addition to their home—a simple and elegant structure that takes full advantage of the dramatic views to the surrounding redwoods and the city basin and hills beyond.

One of the most noteworthy features of the building is its creative use of **art glass** throughout. Although none of the views is undesirable, by using art glass, Morimoto enhanced and framed them in a variety of ways to create a unique lens

through which to see the surroundings. It's as though one were inside a crystal, with the ability to look out through a multitude of facets.

Morimoto used three elements in each window Composition. First, each has a particular leading pattern, or muntin pattern, to divide the view into smaller segments. Second, a range of glass translucencies is used, from almost opaque to completely clear. And third, the position of the

With glass accordion doors (at right) closed, the main social space is clearly "interior." The small panes help to increase the sense of enclosure.

The pool house is designed to work as either an indoor or an outdoor space, depending on the weather.

When the accordion doors are opened all the way, the pool house serves as a sheltered outdoor social space.

translucent segments in relationship to the viewing area has been carefully considered. In some windows, for example, there is no obstruction to the long views, other than the Simple Pattern Overlay (see the photo at right). In others, there is only a little obstruction that modulates the view, in this case to the surrounding redwoods. Because of the use of tiny squares of etched translucent glass in the window shown below, your eye is given two planes to focus on—the plane of the window and the view of the trees. Both the windows and the view seem to gain something by the existence of the other. In combination, they create an interplay that delights the spirit in a way that neither could alone.

Turning 90 degrees in the same room to the window that looks into a bank of bushes directly adjacent to the building, you'll see that the long views aren't present (see the top photo on the facing page). Instead, there's a backdrop of fairly dense foliage, and the etched glass is used in this location to modulate the sameness of the leaf pattern. The effect of the three milky-white squares of

The windows in the curved stair tower that leads down to the lower level have a simple pattern overlay of small panes. The view is unobstructed, but the grid breaks it down into bite-size pieces.

This set of windows in the lower-level gymnasium has smaller panes of different shapes, sizes, and transparencies at the lower edges, which modulates the view.

In a tiny alcove off the gymnasium, a simple tri-partite design provides an art glass focus as you enter the room from the hallway.

Modulating the View

There are times when the view is beautiful, but you want to use the window not only to see out of but also as a backdrop for some transparent art glass. The colors and textures of the vegetation, landscape, or streetscape beyond then become the coloring mechanism for the glass. Although this technique is not used frequently today due to the expense of art glass, it was a favorite technique of Frank Lloyd Wright's, as well as of many of the architects of the Arts and Crafts movement.

Wright would develop a unique graphic pattern for each house, repeating it, with variations in each of the home's windows. The views remain powerful presences in every room, but they are enhanced by the intricate patterning of each window's design, bringing the focus back to the membrane between inside and out. Most of the glass you can see through clearly, but here and there the view is obscured, creating a wonderful and exhilarating shift in focus from the close-up surface to the distant horizon.

glass at the top of the Composition is to allow only shadows of the adjacent leaves to be seen, while the "seedy" glass beneath (glass filled with tiny bubbles) simply softens the focus on the leaves and flowers. Because these two types of glass are used in the main viewing part of the window, your eye is led to focus more on the window than on the view beyond. The window pattern becomes the feature, and the plantings behind become the coloring system. And this coloring changes from hour to hour and from season to season, depending on the quality of the sunlight and the life cycle of the vegetation.

Both windows provide light for a small gymnasium on the lower level of the pool house. This room is heavily influenced by Mackintosh's architectural style, as is the bathroom, which serves as a changing room for both the pool and the gym. Although there are no windows in the bathroom, you can see echoes of patterns used on both lower

In the gymnasium, the window to the left obscures a little more of the view in and out than the one on the right. Even a small amount of translucent glass makes a difference. The focus becomes the window itself, rather than the view beyond.

The bathroom has no windows, but it still feels integrated with the rest of the building's design because of the repetition of patterns used elsewhere in the pool house.

and upper levels of the building. Everything in the pool house is integrated, though the lower level appears to have a very different character from the upper one.

On the upper level, the aesthetics are still recognizably influenced by Mackintosh, but here the expression takes a more Arts and Crafts character. It's really an amalgam of the two styles. Looking toward the fireplace, you see the windows on either side frame the views beyond in different ways. To the left, the window is a stationary unit that overlays a complementary pattern to the shape of the tree trunk beyond. To the right, the window is the first segment of the accordion doors that allow the entire pool house to be opened to the outdoors. As a finishing touch, two subtle art-glass light fixtures have been integrated into the columns flanking the fireplace. Their rose design is a famous Mackintosh signature.

The window above the wet bar is the only ungridded window in the building. Focused on a wonderful old oak tree, it clearly demonstrates the difference in experience between looking through a window with a grid of small panes and one without.

In the main social space, the art-glass window to the left of the fireplace is one point of focus , while the simple grid of small panes to the right focuses attention on the view beyond.

On the opposite side of the room, an elegantly designed wet bar reveals what **small panes** and more complex patterns of glass can do to a view. The small panes make a somewhat plain view seem much more interesting, but when combined with the adjacent broad expanse of unobstructed view, the effect is riveting. The small-paned windows function as a frame for the primary view of the tree.

Once again, we see that contrast, in this case between a tempered view and an unobstructed view, allows us to appreciate more powerfully a feature that is already impressive. There's a sense of moreness that is created by being given the opportunity to see through different window patterns and glass types. The subliminal comparison gives us a richer level of experience, which is the true art of architecture.

PART THREE

Order

MANY PEOPLE DELIGHT IN ORGANIZATION, SEEKING "A PLACE for everything, and everything in its place." This is how we bring order to our "stuff." But there's another kind of order that's less visible, yet just as important to the sense of home. Architects use this more hidden type of order in their designs to arrange all the forms, spaces, and surfaces, just as you might organize the papers on your desk or the spices in your kitchen cabinet. But where on a desk surface you might stack papers based on urgency, or in a spice cabinet you might locate the bottles alphabetically, with space, the organizing strategies used have more to do with visual or experiential characteristics like alignments, rhythms, and geometries.

If we can't find an order to what we're looking at or experiencing, we perceive it as chaos. It's the underlying order that makes a home (or any other type of building) intelligible, and that allows us to feel both safe and comfortable there.

TWENTY

Pattern and Geometry

Adding a pattern to a surface or form helps break it into smaller pieces that make it more intelligible to the eye.

Throughout the ages, architects, artists, builders, and craftspeople have used geometrical patterns to adorn buildings both inside and out. Though not a necessary feature for function or structural integrity, the presence of applied patterning often dramatically and positively affects the experience of those who visit or use the building.

As a young architecture student, I had the opportunity to visit the Alhambra, a thirteenth-century palace/citadel in southern Spain. I was delighted by the extraordinary beauty of the buildings there. Not only were many of the surfaces stunningly decorated with geometrical designs, but even the floor plans were based on patterns extruded into three-dimensional forms.

The experience of being surrounded by such beauty inspired me to identify the characteristics of architectural design that have the power to transport us beyond the mundane to a glimpse of the sacredness in all things. Geometrical pattern has this potential. Frank Lloyd Wright was deeply aware of this when he designed a special signature pattern for each of his buildings, which was expressed in the stained-glass windows, carpets, and other decorative elements. So enchanting are these patterns that today they appear on everything from placemats to key rings. Wright may be turning in his grave, but the beauty of what he created lives on.

Fortunately, you don't need anything so intricate for patterning to provide inspiration and beauty. The Japanese shoji screen, with its simple rectangular divisions, lends a sense of order and balance to a space, as does a garden trellis, with its equally spaced slats. These are very basic geometries, yet they speak to us in a way that surface absent of pattern does not.

Simple Pattern Overlay

A surface that's flat and undifferentiated can look pretty boring, especially if it is overhead, where there's no chance to hang a picture. In such situations, overlaying a simple pattern can help break the surface into bite-size pieces. The pattern makes the plain more intelligible as well as more interesting.

In the attic space shown here, there'd be much less sense of scale without the pattern made of batten strips across the low ceiling surface. The regular rhythm of the battens allows you to perceive the approximate length of the space. Without the pattern overlay the length of the room would be ambiguous. Of course, there are practical advantages to this strategy as well. For example, you can finish the ceiling with 4x8 sheets of plywood and cover the seams with the batten strips.

Plain versus Patterned

When I'm designing a house, I often use a simple pattern overlay on the garage doors to make them look more interesting. To me, metal garage doors look cheap and they feel industrial. So when I have a client who wants a nice-looking door but doesn't have the money for a paneled one or for a custom-designed one, I'll specify a plain wood or high-density fiberboard door, with a simple pattern added to it with 1x4s or 1x6s. This inexpensive

trick makes the garage door more distinct and personal. In fact, you can get quite creative with the design, but my favorite approach is to keep it simple but elegant, as Seattle architect Frank Karreman has done here.

Grilles and Lattices

Another way to use geometric pattern is to filter the view from one place to another through a lattice or grille. This strategy superimposes a pattern over what lies beyond, which helps obscure or screen the view while simultaneously giving us something interesting to look at in the foreground. We are most familiar with this idea in the garden, where a trellis or pergola can shade an outdoor patio. The lattice in this case separates the sitting space from the sky above, by creating a see-through ceiling. From the patio beneath there is a strong sense of Shelter around Activity, yet there is also connection to above.

In our culture, we rarely use lattices on the interior of the house, though they can add a beautiful and delicate quality to a room. In Japanese architecture, grilles and lattices are often used to partially screen a view. The allure of the partially visible is a little like a fine veil. We know the screen is there to obscure the view, but it makes what lies beyond all the more intriguing. When this is combined with a particularly delightful geometric pattern the effect is even more entrancing.

Geometric Feature

You can use a geometric pattern feature in all sorts of ways in a house. A geometric arrangement of doors and drawers can be made into a single focal element, like the wall unit shown here that combines fireplace, TV, stereo equipment, and storage for videos, tapes, CDs, and DVDs. Or a geometric relationship can be used as a sort of graphic signature throughout the house, like the combination of squares into patterns of fours and nines shown in the photo below. Though the patterns appear in various materials, sometimes as a lattice, sometimes as a window, and sometimes as a light fixture, the formation is always the same— either two times two, or three times three, weaving a wonderful continuity of expression wherever you go in the house. You can read more about this house and its patterns in Chapter 23, Theme and Variations.

Pattern Feature

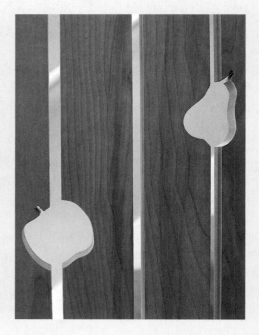

A pattern can also be something more organic, more personal, or even whimsical. In this 1910 bungalow, the stairway is a playful combination of convention and whimsy, with a variety of fruit forms cut into the vertical boards of the railing design. Although the boards themselves create a geometric expression, as in most railings, the pattern feature here is the organic form of the fruit.

I've seen all sorts of shapes used to make a stair railing more interesting—everything from fish to leaves to golf clubs. It's a great place to make a fun personal statement. Remember, though, if the house will ever be sold, the decoration will need to have a universal appeal. There's also a fine line between delightful self-expression and over-the-top kitsch, so be careful. If you're not sure, check it out with a friend or two first.

Bridging Old and New

ELISSA MORGANTE and Frederick Wilson, a husband and wife who are both architects in the Chicago area, took a classic 1928 home and turned it into an unusually successful marriage of traditional and contemporary design styles. To fit into the older neighborhood, they left the exterior mostly in tact, changing only the entry by removing the gabled roof over the front door and replacing it with a sheltering trellis instead. But once inside, the house is full of details that, although by no means typical of the style of the original house, still work well, helping to bridge the differences between the more formal character of an older home and the informality of today's lifestyle.

The living room is the first space you step into as you move through the front door, and you are immediately greeted by a **geometric feature**—the stair railing, which in this home is composed of tightly spaced square spindles. The railing creates a

3-ft.-high lattice through which you can glimpse the arched opening to the family room beyond. As you explore the house further, you discover that geometric Pattern is apparent at every turn, even in something as basic as the arrangement of photos on the upper stair wall. Although the photos appear random at first glance, on closer inspection you'll see that they are loosely aligned with one another to give an overall order to a mix of frame sizes for a collection of images documenting the

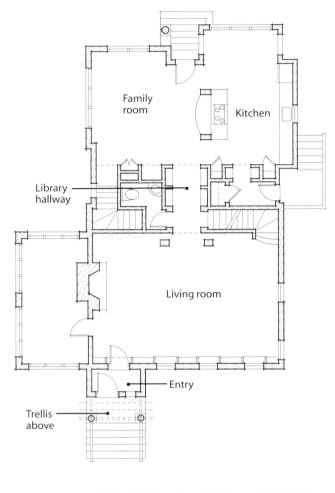

This house in the suburbs of Chicago looks simple enough on the outside, but there are plenty of geometrical surprises inside.

family's history. (For anyone who's lived or worked with an architect, you'll know that we tend to be obsessive about this sort of thing.)

To get to the new part of the house, the kitchen and family room, you have to pass through a tunnel of sorts, a book-lined hallway that marks the transition between the formal and informal parts of the house (see the bottom photo on p. 184). Here, we are looking back through the hallway from the family room side. The ceiling is gently curved, which is brought to your attention with a **simple pattern overlay**—a double batten strip every 3 ft., which continues down the edges of the book shelf dividers as an articulated column. There's even a subtle pattern in the flooring, a series of inlaid maple squares that further indicate the threshold between public and private zones. Although none

Geometrical patterns, from the tightly spaced lattice of spindles in the handrail to the collection of family photos on the wall behind, give the house a strong sense of order.

In the master bedroom, a simple pattern overlay of wood battens creates a ribbed effect on the ceiling, which helps to define its gently curving form. This geometric feature is accentuated by the use of a slightly different color for the battens and headband than for the ceiling surface itself.

The book-lined hallway between the formal and informal areas of the house has several layers of patterning visible, from the march of the columns between aligned shelves to the grid of light wood squares inlaid in the darker floor.

The character of the kitchen is largely defined by the playful cabinet doors, which are used as a canvas for a geometrical work of art reminiscent of a Mondrian painting.

Grilles and lattices can be used as effective space dividers without completely separating the rooms on either side.

of these visual cues is critical to the success of the hallway, in combination they embellish the transition and make it a celebrated event rather than just a matter of movement.

The architects used a similar batten technique in their bedroom. The ceiling here didn't need to be curved, but Elissa points out that you tend to look at the ceiling far more in a bedroom than in most rooms, so why not make it something beautiful and interesting? The batten strips follow the form of the ceiling and are painted a subtly different color to draw your eye to the curvature. This **pattern feature** recalls that of the library hallway and also gives the bedroom more personality.

The most pronounced geometric patterns in the house are apparent only from the kitchen. Here, both the cabinetry and the divider between the kitchen and the family room have been carefully composed to provide a geometrical feast for the eyes. Although at first the lines in the cabinetry

appear random, they are actually subtle indicators of Alignments with other objects and forms in the room. (Remember what I told you about architects?) In the photo shown at left above, the alignment that's most clearly related to something else is the one between the dark walnut line that runs all the way across the upper cabinets and the center muntin in the upper window sash.

The room divider is cleverly designed to allow easy sight and communication between cook and other family members, while still providing a significant screening for the work area. Although you can see through the divider quite clearly, it accomplishes its screening function by providing something of much greater interest in the foreground that arrests the eye and stops you from exploring further into the space. Remove the screen, though, and the rest of the kitchen would be on show.

TWENTY-ONE

Alignments

When two adjacent or related elements are lined up with one another,
there's a sense of order and quality to the space they are part of.

WHEN YOU STAND AT THE SINK in a powder room, you expect the mirror to be centered directly above it. When you look at the gable end of a house, you expect to see the windows centered under the ridge. We have very definite expectations about what should align with what, and how, but because we don't often talk about these things, we only find out what those expectations are when they aren't met, which can be very frustrating, as well as expensive to remedy.

A few years ago when I was on a construction visit to a house I had designed, the project was close to completion and the security and smoke alarm system had been installed just the day before. As I walked through the house, I noticed that the smoke detectors had been placed quite arbitrarily on the ceiling with no regard to the location of other features in the room. So, in one hallway where all the recessed lights marched in perfect order along its centerline, the smoke detector sat a good 4 in. off center. It would have been simple to align it with the light fixtures, making it a part of the overall Composition. But the installer hadn't thought about it so instead the smoke detector stood out like a sore thumb.

The moral of the story is that if you want one element to align with another, you have to say so before construction starts, and the ideal place for this is on the blueprints. Just because *you* would automatically line things up in a certain way doesn't mean that everyone working in the house will see it the same way. How much easier it would be if we had some language to describe the Alignments that are important to us before construction starts. The applications that follow should help you to do just that.

Perfect Symmetry

Partial Symmetry

When something is perfectly symmetrical, we could draw a line down the center and everything on one side would be the exact mirror image of what's on the other side. Sometimes we'll want a view to have a quality of perfection to it, and here perfect symmetry is appropriate.

In the connecting opening between the dining room and kitchen shown here, the view through the opening is really the focal point of the room, so the architect has organized all the visible elements on either side of the opening to be perfectly aligned with one another. Now, imagine if the hanging light fixture on the dining room side were mounted off center. It would look like a mistake for sure. In this kind of situation, once you've committed to a symmetrical design, you need to carry it through to its logical conclusion. But the rest of the kitchen and the rest of the dining room don't need to be symmetrical as well. It's important to know when enough is enough.

We generally think of our faces as symmetrical, but if you hold a mirror up against its centerline, lining it up with your nose, you'll quickly realize that this isn't really so. It's close but not exact. This is true throughout nature. Symmetry is typically approximate about a centerline, but not perfect. Architects will often line up a major building element, like the fireplace shown here, with the centerline of a room, but will do something quite different on either side of that central object. Everything that's associated with the centered fireplace, however, is perfectly symmetrical. If it weren't the space would look very odd. It would be like having your nose off center on your face. There's symmetry, but there's also variation and interest generated by the differences that occur to either side. Overall, the composition is balanced.

What the Eye Sees One of my first projects as an architect was an addition to a simple Colonial home. A key part of weaving the new structure into the old was the intersection of three pathways in the house. During construction, we discovered that some existing plumbing prevented one of the pathways from aligning perfectly with the other two. I was disappointed but resigned to the fact that the intersection wouldn't look as elegant as I'd originally hoped.

But to my surprise, when the house was finished, you couldn't tell that the alignments weren't perfect. I had learned an important lesson. What looks aligned in three dimensions doesn't always look perfect on the floor plan.

Asymmetry

Sometimes asymmetry is highly desirable. It would be a boring world indeed if everything were symmetrical. But just as with a design that's partially symmetrical, it's important to create a sense of balance with all the constituent parts of a composition even when it is asymmetrical.

A good example is shown in the photo above. This home was remodeled and a new curved ceiling added. The problem was that once the curved ceiling was in place, the door at the far end of the hall looked seriously off center. To correct the situation and return the entire composition to balance, a rug was designed that redefined the center of the space. If you look carefully, you'll see that there's a dark brown band that runs around the perimeter of the carpet; but on the left-hand side there's an additional gray strip whose right-hand side is exactly the same distance from the center of the door to that of the brown band on the right-hand side of the hall. The eye is subtly conned into believing that the door is in fact centered on something. It now looks balanced. Although one would normally never stop and figure this out, the effect doesn't require the intellect to be successful. The eye sees it as balanced, which is all that matters.

View along a Main Axis

The alignment of views is particularly important when there is a strong visual axis from one place to another. This is one of the primary reasons why the principle of Light to Walk Toward is so powerful.

A common location for a long view through the house is from the front entry. Although it is by no means necessary to have a view all the way from one side of the house to the other, this is sometimes a design strategy used to capture our attention as we stand at the door. In the house shown here, there's a dramatic view straight through the house from the front entry to the large picture window on the opposite side, overlooking the ocean. Imagine how much less impressive the view would have been if it were bisected by a window mullion. When we can connect the visitor's gaze to the horizon line several miles beyond the opposite side of the house, it gives the sense that the house is a sort of prism for appreciating the surrounding views.

If In Doubt, Line It Up

There are many places in a house where things look better when they are aligned with one another. In this bathroom, for example, there are four separate elements that all fall into line with one another at the vanity area.

First, there is the window, which aligns with the raised section of vanity that defines a distinct activity area—a small articulation of Shelter around Activity for the sink area. Then, there's the light shelf above that crosses the room and ends at the window. The shelf is the same width as the window so that the alignment looks effortless. And finally the wood trim that flanks the light shelf continues on around the room at the same height. If any one of these elements had been out of alignment by even 1 in., the whole composition would have looked awkward.

What isn't typically understood is that for these things to be built this way, someone has to explain to the builder how all the materials are to come together. That's the role of a design professional.

Half a Bubble Off

When you have an asymmetrical composition, you have a little more latitude about alignments. Because your eye recognizes that things are not exactly the same on one side of a view as on the other, it isn't so critical that the object at the center be absolutely centered, while in a symmetrical situation it *is* critical.

Look at the window at the bottom of the stairway shown above, for example. The window does not perfectly align with the stair landing. It's actually "half a bubble off" to the right. But because the left side of the stairway is so different from the right side as you are facing the window, your eye doesn't object.

Imagine, however, if the doorway in the very symmetrical dining room shown at right were the same amount off center to the right as the window in the example above. It would look terrible. So, in general, with an asymmetrical Composition, being half a bubble off looks just fine, whereas in a symmetrical situation it doesn't.

Line It Up

THIS HOME, which we've looked at before in the chapters on Ceiling Height Variety and Reflecting Surfaces, has one over-arching principle at play in its design. In whichever direction you choose to look, there are objects, walls, windows, or columns in the distance that perfectly align with something close at hand. If you look at the floor plan on p. 192, you'll quickly see that there is a very strong sense of symmetry around both the axes running through the living room—the one that runs the length of the room and the one that runs across its width—

This Minnesota home features symmetrical alignments in every direction. Here, in a view along the main axis of the house, the triangular windows at either end are in perfect alignment.

The ridge of the roof defines the centerline of the dining room/sunroom wing, and the walls flanking the dividing buffet frame the square window at the middle of the sunroom.

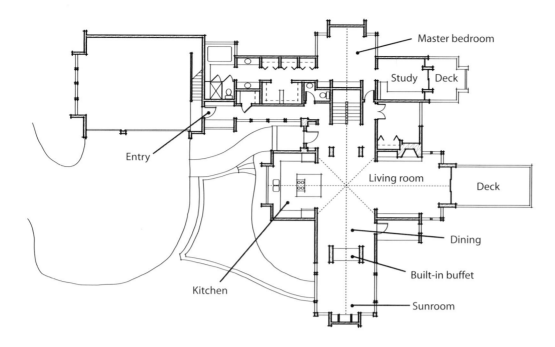

Entry

Master bedroom

Study Deck

Living room

Deck

Dining

Built-in buffet

Kitchen

Sunroom

The strong sense of symmetry extends into the master bedroom, where the bed is tucked into a shallow alcove beneath another triangular window.

connecting the dining room and sunroom on one arm with the piano alcove, stairway, and master bedroom on the other. In many ways, this is a house designed around the application, view along a main axis.

The **symmetry** of the long living room axis starts on the deck to the living room and extends all the way through to the kitchen at the other end of the space. The other axis is just as symmetrical, though more segmented. So, as you look toward the sun room from the center of the living room, you see a perfectly centered table (with a diamond-shaped base that recalls the triangular forms of the ceilings throughout the house); **perfectly symmetrical** wing walls on either side of the built-in buffet, and wide window mullions beyond that not only align with the wing walls but are also exactly the same thickness. All these building elements are also perfectly aligned with the ridge of the cathedral ceiling above. A misalignment of any one of these elements would have looked like a serious mistake.

Looking in the opposite direction, from the sunroom back through the dining and living rooms to the piano alcove and stairway beyond, there's a similar set of Alignments. But here the bottles on the buffet and the shape of the piano alleviate the predictability of the symmetry. These freestanding and movable elements add personality to the space by breaking the rigidity of the pattern. A piano, by its very nature, is not symmetrical, and its form has a particular, asymmetrical beauty to it. The bottles are placed on the right-hand side of the opening, where they emphasize the flow of the piano's form.

These are subtle relationships, but as you become sensitive to design and balance, you'll

In this view across the built-in buffet, it's clear that the alignments along the centerline continue all the way from the sunroom to the stairway wall.

Asymmetry in Balance

Asymmetry can be used very intentionally. In the house shown here, this library space has a great deal of asymmetry, but also a real sense of balance. The ridge of the vaulted ceiling does not define the center of the room, and the bookshelves aren't centered on the room or the ridge beam. Even the beam to the right of the picture is not related to the window beneath it. Yet visually everything seems in harmony.

What makes this composition work is the presence of the bright window, which balances the darker visual mass of the bookshelves. One balances out the other, and one's eye is quite willing to enjoy the interplay of forms. If you were to remove the windows, however, the room would seem too heavily weighted to the left. It loses some of its balance.

start to be more aware of the invisible connections and tensions between all the shapes and objects in a space. You can think of this as spatial poetry. Just as there's no "right" way to position words within a poem, there's no precise rule to follow with respect to the positioning of building elements. However, there is an ineffable "something" that gets conveyed through these interrelationships.

At the opposite side of the house from the sunroom is the master bedroom, with the bed centered on the back wall of the axis that crosses the living room. It sits in a shallow alcove that's crowned by an equilateral triangle, the Signature Form for this home. Even if there were room,

positioning the bed on a different wall would not be in keeping with the poetry of the house.

Although we may not be conscious of the relationship of the bed's positioning to the whole house, at a subliminal level we can feel it. When architects design a house, or any other type of building, they are almost always aware of these subtle, hidden relationships that are expressed through the three-dimensional layout. If you're working with an architect, and you'd like to know if there is any such embedded poetry in what he or she has designed for you, just ask. Most will be more than happy to tell you about it.

TWENTY-TWO

Rhythm

Many of the materials used in making a house have a natural rhythm to them, and these can be combined to create a home that's far more than just an assemblage of parts.

MANY OF THE ORGANIZING CRITERIA that allow us to appreciate music have direct parallels in architecture. Just as in music there is almost always some recognizable Rhythm that provides an ordering system for the sequence of notes, so in architecture there's usually a sequential patterning of one or more elements that creates an underlying rhythm.

Think about some classic house styles, and you'll have a sense of what I'm describing. The standard Colonial, for example, has a very straightforward rhythm, usually composed of five or seven windows equally spaced across its face on the upper level, with the same pattern of windows on the main level, except at the center where a front door is substituted. If one of the windows were even a few inches out of alignment with the others, the rhythm would be thrown off, and the facade would look out of balance.

The same is true for a house with a porch that stretches the full width of the front. The equally spaced porch columns provide a strong, clear Rhythm and balance that's easily understood. I think at least part of the reason these uncomplicated forms have such lasting appeal is their predictability, just as the tempo of a march or a waltz is to our ears.

But Rhythm in architecture can be far more sophisticated. Rhythms are established by the various materials used in a house—such as windows, siding, bricks, and rafters—and these interpenetrate to create complex patterns and harmonies. One of the real arts of good residential design derives from the orchestration of these different rhythms into a composition that looks and feels effortless both inside and out without compromising function in the process.

The March

The Triad

A lot of the structural materials used in building are organized in a repetitive pattern. Think about the joists, studs, and rafters that make up the skeleton of a house, for example. All these members are spaced consistently apart—usually at either 16 in. or 24 in. on center. When they are exposed, as in the house shown here, they produce a strong Rhythm as they march across the surface they support. When they are combined with an overhead light source, like this skylight, or a difference in color between the ceiling surface and the rafters themselves, attention is focused on the rhythmic presence of the structural members in question.

The word "march" is a perfect description for the order they bring to the architecture, just like the musical form of the same name. Stairs are another element that bear this precisely spaced pattern. In general, any element that is repeated too many times to easily comprehend the number present is a march.

A rhythm you'll see frequently when you start looking for it is the use of three elements of the same size and shape, placed adjacent to one another. Along the stairway shown above, for example, there are three equally spaced windows. From the outside, you can't see the staircase, but you can enjoy the triad of windows that tell you what is almost certainly going on inside at this point in the structure. If only two windows were used, the effect would be less dramatic, and might even look like a mistake. But when three are used in succession, there's a deliberateness to the action that makes you understand that the visual effect was intentional.

Another aspect of the triad is organizing the elements in direct horizontal or vertical alignment. The middle part, then, takes on added importance since it is flanked on each side. The sides are like sentinels that focus attention on the center. You'll often see a triad of identically shaped openings, with the center one housing a TV or fireplace, for example, as shown here. In case there is any doubt that the center is the point of focus for the room, the position has been accented further with the wall hanging above.

The Waltz

Rhythmic Refrain

There are other patterns of building elements that have parallels to musical forms. For example, a waltz has a series of three counts per measure, whose Rhythm is repeated over and over, usually with a stronger accent on the first note in each set of three. (Think of Johann Strauss's *Blue Danube Waltz* in the movie *2001: A Space Odyssey*.)

Shown above is an example of the architectural equivalent of the waltz, where every third rafter supporting the trellised sunscreen is longer and beefier than the others, to encase a scupper allowing rainwater to drain off the flat roof above. There are undoubtedly architectural examples of other musical forms as well, like the polka, the two-step, and the samba. Although architects don't normally refer to their design patterns by this terminology, perhaps if we began to do so, it would open up all sorts of new visual rhythms in the built environment. When you name something, you start to see the form more clearly and to use it in your own creations.

A refrain is something that is repeated wherever there is a particular type of experience that you want to draw attention to. Many older homes employ a rhythmic refrain of sorts in the muntin patterns of windows and doorways, to emphasize the transitions between inside and outside and the passageways between rooms.

In the remodeling shown above, the architect used this approach to mark the entrances between activity areas. A sequence of small square openings and narrow muntins appears at the top of almost every framed opening. They can be thought of as a rhythmic refrain, subliminally reminding you that you are leaving one space and entering another. Such a refrain could also be rendered as a pattern of trim work at the corners of each room, for example, or as a tile pattern on one or both sides of every exterior door.

A similar configuration has been used in the contemporary home shown above to draw attention to the glass surface without obstructing the view. Notice the difference when the rhythmic refrain is removed. Although neither version is better than the other, the effects of the two approaches are dramatically different.

Frozen Music

S OMETIMES WHEN an architect works on a new home or remodel, the client makes a unique request that helps personalize the home to his or her particular passions and life experiences. Such was the case with this rambler remodel. The client, a violinist of Japanese heritage, asked James Childress, a partner with Centerbrook Architects in Connecticut, if he could redesign her home to let in more light and view, while at the same time in some way recall the shapes and forms of the musical instrument that so colored her life. What Childress came up with was a remodel that left the existing roof and walls in tact but gave the home a very different interior character and window configuration.

By introducing some curved canvas ceiling forms in the new great room interior, Childress was able to evoke a simple reference to the violin's natural and beautiful curves. But in addition to the musical references, he also wanted to honor

In the main living area, a series of equally spaced columns and beams support fabric ceiling "clouds" that define the activity places beneath. The sliding doors and windows beyond beat out the same simple march in double time.

This simple ranch house was dramatically remodeled on its interior to reflect the lyrical tastes of its owner, a musician with a passion for Japanese design.

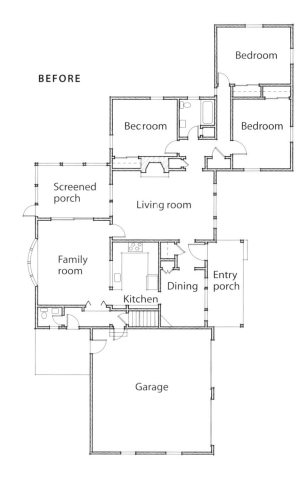

BEFORE

Bedroom

Bedroom

Bedroom

Screened porch

Living room

Family room

Dining

Entry porch

Kitchen

Garage

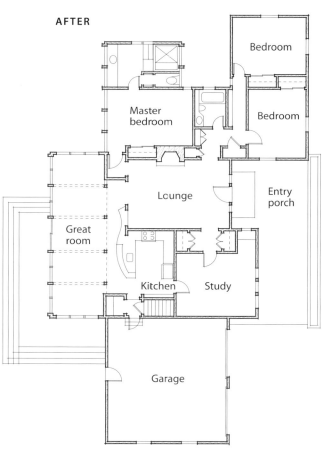

AFTER

Bedroom

Master bedroom

Bedroom

Lounge

Entry porch

Great room

Kitchen

Study

Garage

A separate pavilion on the same property, with three wide windows of equal proportions to those in the main house, serves as a music studio.

ing barn on the property into a music studio. Again the homeowner expressed a desire to continue the same motifs, and again Childress, in collaboration with colleague Stephen Holmes, rose to the task in an inventive way. This time, instead of evoking the forms of the violin with canvas forms, he used curved plywood panels that both shape the room and simultaneously serve an acoustical function (see the photo on p. 194). Their simplicity and elegance is striking. The space feels serene and melodious, even when silent. The building itself is "frozen music," as eighteenth-century author and poet Goethe so aptly observed about good architecture.

But the reason for including these two structures in this chapter on rhythm is obvious. Both are colored by a bold interplay of rhythms—perhaps the most prominent feature of the designs. In the main dwelling, the face of the house that looks out to the backyard is composed of five segments, three containing sliding doors, and the other two containing sliding windows of the same width. This is essentially the Rhythm and order we discussed in the application named **the triad.** Focus is brought to the center section, which contains a slightly wider door, by the flanking window segments and separating columns. So this centerpiece can afford to be a different size without looking odd. If one of

the owner's culture of origin. The redesigned interior has a subtly Japanese flavor, without resorting to classically traditional forms. There's a characteristic simplicity to the organization of spaces and materials that recalls the elegance of Japanese aesthetics, but with a contemporary Western flair.

In 2000, six years after the house was finished, the client returned with a request to turn an exist-

Rhythms within Rhythms In many situations there is more than one rhythm at play in a design. For example, in the pool house shown here, several different building elements have been applied in a rhythmic way.

First, there is the perfectly spaced pattern of trusses that march across the room. The rigidity of the form, however, has been softened by the curving midsection members that make them appear more lilting and melodic than a typical march. Then there are the parallel lines of overhead lamps, which create a different sense of order because they are round, not linear. Finally, the glass accordion doors produce a strong rhythm that's modulated by the metal grid of smaller squares. In combination, all these rhythms produce an elegant visual symphony that stirs the heart in ways we may not fully understand but can certainly feel.

At the back of the house, the widely spaced verticals between the sliding doors and windows define a steady march. The center mullions divide the rhythm into half beats.

the other segments were the larger one, however, the composition would look off to the eye.

In addition to the pronounced **march** of the window mullions and beams above, there's also a subordinate rhythm created by the ornamental window divider that bisects each of the large transom windows above the sliding doors and windows. These are essentially the architectural equivalents of half notes, with the resulting Rhythm that looks like the following sound pattern: Daa di Daa di Daa di Daa di Daa. The rhythm of these elements can be appreciated from both outside and inside. But on the inside there is an additional reinforcement of the Daa's— the window mullions—with the line of columns that separate the living space from the kitchen and entryway. Notice how the vertical supports for the canvas

The sequence of columns provides a suggestion of a wall between kitchen, dining, and living areas, without obstructing the views between them.

"clouds" above are a double beat that sandwich the beam—again a triadic expression. All these elements are applied rhythmically, and the resulting composition has a distinctly musical quality to it as a result.

The rhythms in the music studio are just as pronounced, but there, in addition to the pattern of window mullions and beam extensions above, the interior clouds themselves have a rhythm. The supports are invisible, but the clouds are equally spaced with respect to each other. The delicate hanging light fixtures reiterate the rhythm in a different material (see the photo on p. 194). And with a final triadic flourish, the round window at the end wall of the room has been ornamented with a randomly spaced sequence of three verticals. This room, which is a very good example of spatial music, illustrates the parallels between architecture and music. It embodies Rhythm, balance, and harmony and results in a melodious composition of great beauty.

TWENTY-THREE

Theme and Variations

A house needs some repeating feature or features to provide a theme of forms, colors, or materials, which then tie all the disparate parts together into a single expression.

A FEW YEARS AGO, a local high-end builder in the Minneapolis/St. Paul area attempted an innovative marketing approach. The company invited a number of prominent interior designers from the area to decorate one of their most impressive spec houses. Each designer was given a room and was allowed to decorate it however he or she wished. The idea was interesting but the result was a house where every room was a solo-flight creative extravaganza, with no relationship to anything else in the house. Without some features that were recognizably similar from room to room there was no sense of continuity and no sense that this was a single home with a definable character.

When a house is fairly mundane in its basic design, you can develop a theme and variations through furnishings and decor as many people do. But you can also do this through the design of the house itself. Many older homes, for example, have a theme and variations developed through the use of wainscoting and crown moldings in each of the primary living spaces. Although the wainscoting may extend higher up the wall in some rooms than in others and the crown molding may have a different profile from one room to the next, the application of these trim materials helps develop a character for the house. It has a theme, and as you move from room to room these features weave the house together.

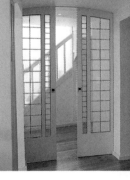

If you want a house to have a greater sense of integrity, there are many materials, forms, colors, and patterns that can help establish a Theme and Variations, as the examples in this chapter show. When you apply this principle, the house gains a connectedness and continuity throughout, and a melody all its own.

Signature Form

One of the simplest and most common themes in house design is the use of a repeated form, which becomes its primary identifying characteristic. In the example shown here, the architect used arches to weave a Spanish flavor throughout the house. The arched forms are not exact replicas, but our eye makes the connection that they are all relatives of each other. With a signature form you can either repeat the form exactly or make variations on the theme established by the form. Even the high ceiling of the living room is gently arched, and the form is brought to our attention with the use of large beams of a strongly contrasting color. Taken together, the three arches we see in these two images clearly identify them as parts of one composition, one home.

Archetypal Form

One other strategy that ties a house to a larger geometrical theme is to use an archetypal form, like a square, a circle, or an equilateral triangle, to decorate a house. These forms have a perfection to them that subliminally connects us to the movements of the cosmos. A perfect square suggests the order of earth, manifestation, and the four directions of the compass; an equilateral triangle subliminally reminds us of the spiritual trinity, which appears in many different religions as a fundamental relationship between self, spirit, and higher power; and a circle connects us with the cosmos and the unity of everything as parts of one "Beingness."

This theme relates the house to the greater wonders of the universe it resides in. One of my favorite quotes from Plato is "God is a geometer." When you see archetypal forms like the circular window shown here, you can feel that truth. Whether or not you believe in God as a definable entity, architecture can connect us directly to the ineffable and essential qualities of our extraordinary universe.

Signature Pattern

Another way to give a house a theme with variations is to repeat an easily recognizable pattern in a number of places, both inside and out. This was more commonly done 100 years ago than it is today. In the last few years, people have started to recognize the value of repeating a pattern to tie a house together aesthetically and have taken things into their own hands. Stenciling a frieze around the tops of primary rooms is one way to do this. Another is to purchase windows with a particular pattern of muntins.

When a house has many different characters of rooms, this technique can be particularly valuable, as it creates a connection among spaces that share few other characteristics. In the house shown here, different areas of the house sport markedly different design styles. The architect has cleverly woven these disparate pieces together with a repeated pattern—a set of four closely nested squares. Though each "four squares" signature is rendered in a different material to fit the aesthetics of the room in which it appears, the pattern is always the same. Collectively, they give the house a distinct identity. It literally becomes its signature.

Repeated Material

You can also imbue a house with a theme and variations by using the same building material in a variety of different ways. For example, architects and craftspeople often use the same species of wood trim through-out a house or may intermingle two species of wood in the same way consistently.

In the house shown here, the architect used glass block as a repeated material to allow in light but to obscure view. The glass block also gives the house a recognizable theme. Here, 8-in. by 8-in. blocks are used at the front entry sidelight and in the master bathroom shower.

A repeated material doesn't have to be used in the same way every time. The character and modular nature of the material itself is what weaves the connection among spaces and subliminally communicates that these are parts of the same house.

Repeated Relationship

Instead of using the same materials, colors, or patterns, you can sometimes use a repeated relationship between forms and materials to conceptually connect rooms that are really very different in feel.

In this home, which we saw previously in Chapter 16, Reflecting Surfaces, the architect used a dark-paneled ceiling in the main living area and brought the clerestory windows tight up to the underside of this surface so that the visually heavy ceiling almost appears to float. In the library, a room of the same height as the living room, he and his clients decided on a lighter, airier feel and so opted for a white ceiling. However, to tie the house together—to make both rooms very recognizably parts of the same house—the relationship between the clerestory windows and the ceiling surface was retained. The technique successfully associates the two rooms, even though their respective characters are dra-matically different from one another.

Repeated Color

When used creatively, color can bring some additional poetry and meaning to a house, especially if it is used to indicate sim-ilarities among building elements. In the house shown here, the architect chose to identify certain focal points throughout the house with the same strong terra-cotta red. Not only is the eye drawn to the color, but it also subliminally identifies these features as a set. They are woven together by their color coding.

In my own designs, I often use one color for the primary wall surfaces between the baseboard and the headband (if there is one), another for alcoves, walls behind bookshelves and built-ins, and another for focal points like the area above a fireplace. This gives the homeowner, as well as guests, a subtle visual cue as to the type of space they're in. The analogous situation in music occurs when the key signature changes periodically to evoke a different emotion for particular passages.

Playful Repeats

The bold walls of color between windows are a signature form that repeats throughout the house, as are the black-framed windows that hug the adjacent wall and ceiling surfaces. Change the color and you have a room with a very different character.

THIS HOME, designed by Bay Area architect Cathy Schwabe for a single mother and her two teenage children, contains a number of excellent examples of themes and their respective variations. Probably the most notable theme is that of the black highlights against the moody colored plaster and concrete surfaces. This is really a combination of two **repeated colors** and a repeated texture applied to a repeated form. So it also illustrates a **repeated relationship** between color, texture, and form.

The relationship is easiest to see in the living room, where black-framed windows abut a thick, rectangular gray-green plaster wall. The windows are of various widths, but their configuration vertically is always the same—a tall lower window under a short openable transom window, which constitutes a **signature form** for the home. Both the colored wall and the adjacent upper window also directly abut the horizontal ceiling surface with no additional wall surface between. If the windows had wallboard surrounding them, the relationship would be much less compelling. If you were also to remove the color distinctions between elements, the design would look even flatter. The alignment of elements, together with their particular coloring, adds a lot of flavor.

The bold colored wall at the entry is a key feature that ties together all the repeated materials and relationships. It is adorned with a spiral artwork—one of the most recognizable archetypal forms.

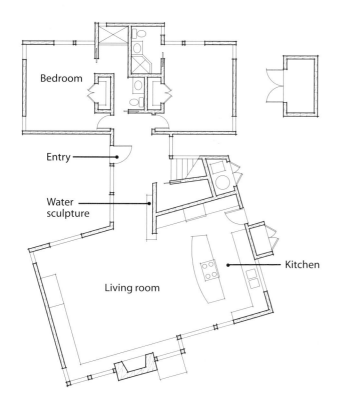

In this house, both the purple and the gray-green colors are used for focal walls. A large purple wall greets you as you first enter the home. The fabric spiral at the center of this surface suggests harmony and gives the home personality. As you move farther into the house, you see the same color in the living room, on the wall behind the couch. And it is reiterated in the master bedroom, behind the bed. The windows in the bedroom butt up against the ceiling and the adjacent colored wall between in just the same way that they do in the family room. This is a perfect illustration of the way a Theme and Variations can be used to identify two different spaces as parts of the same house, without making both exactly the same, and without resorting to conservative colors and textures. Even the artwork selected by the owner reiterates the color selection, giving the room an elegant composition in its own right.

In the entryway, the black highlights are different from those in the bedroom and living room. Here, there's a powerful focal point for the house—an internal fountain sculpture at the base of the purple wall, which fills the main living areas with the serene ambiance of trickling water while helping cool and humidify the warm, dry California air. The water descends to a shallow pool that's recessed below the level of the floor and the

The concrete artwork extends into the floor plane and out beyond the windows into the garden.

Filling the house with the sound of falling water, the concrete fountain at the base of the entry wall sets the stage for the black highlights found throughout the design.

pool's concrete surround. If you look closely, you'll see that this concrete area extends over to the exterior wall, and seems to continue uninterrupted beneath the windows that extend all the way to the floor. It's a good example of a home that has blurred the barrier between inside and out.

Collectively, the themes give the house much of its personality. A Theme and Variations can be a great asset in establishing the mood and character of any home. As this house so aptly illustrates, the themes don't have to be heavy handed but, like the musical concept of the same name, can enhance the bones of the structure and make it something elegantly personal.

The black-framed windows are repeated in the master bedroom. As in the living room, the upper transoms butt against the ceiling, but here the sloped ceiling and overhang beyond give the room a different ambience.

TWENTY-FOUR

Composition

When a house is well composed it looks balanced and attractive from every side (as well as inside), and it has a sense of integrity to it when viewed as a whole.

COMPOSITION IS A WORD that we usually associate with music, art, or writing, but it is just as applicable to architecture and home design. Architects use the term to mean the interrelationship between forms, surfaces, and materials to create an overall design. It can be applied to a whole house, to a single wall surface, or even to a discrete area of that surface, such as the front door and its surrounding features.

When you look at the front face of most new houses they are at least to some degree "composed." Someone has usually thought about the relationships between windows, door, roof, and other elements like shutters and light fixtures and has attempted to make them look good. But move to one side or the other, and there's a very different experience. The sides and back of the house are typically uncomposed, the windows falling where they do because of interior considerations only, with no thought given to how this might look from the outside. Often the siding changes from front to sides as well— for example, from brick to vinyl siding. It's as though the street face belongs to one house, and the other sides to quite another. In other words, there's no sense of the house as a single, integrated whole.

Houses built a century or more ago rarely have this kind of segmentation. The character of the house is sustained on every side, and each face was designed so that windows align from one story to the next and the materials used on the front of the house wrap around to the back. There's no reason a house built today can't have this same kind of integrity. All it takes is an understanding of composition—of how to relate the various building elements to each other.

Balance

Window Composition

Attaining visual balance is easy when a composition is symmetrical. Basically, everything on one side of the design perfectly mimics and reflects what's on the opposite side. But when a Composition is markedly asymmetrical, the challenge is significantly greater to create visual balance. Here, there must be something of equivalent visual weight introduced on one side to balance the visual weight of the other side.

In the room shown here, there's a cozy eating area with a lowered ceiling—a soffit—extending across its left side, which is an extension of the adjacent kitchen soffit. This soffit produces a powerful sense of movement through the space, almost like an arrow pointing to the back wall. The homeowners sensed the strength of this movement and placed a dark-colored plate on the wall

below, as though to mark the bull's eye where the arrow has landed. But the architect has provided his own visual balance as well—a vaulted ceiling, culminating in a high triangular window, which perfectly balances the strength of the low soffit on the left.

Just as you find the point of balance on a traditional two-sided scale by adding and removing ever smaller weights, in design you use the same approach. You start with some pretty strong, broad gestures, like the soffit and the vaulted ceiling in this image, and then balance them with some smaller elements, like the plate and the triangular window. Removing the plate and the upper window dramatically alters the sense of balance, as you can see from the photo above.

The windows in a house, whether seen from the inside or from the outside, provide a very important anchor both for the composition of the surface they inhabit and for the interior space they're a part of. You can give every side of the house a composed and intentional appearance by placing the windows to create visual balance, but you can also give each set of windows a personality of its own.

Windows don't have to be ganged together in the normal configurations of two, three, four, and five units of equal dimension. (For more on this see the sidebar on p. 217.) In the house shown here, the architect took the opportunity to make a grouping of windows into a special composition that adds a lot not only to the room but also to the home's exterior. An occasional focal window composition like this can transform an average house into something unique and inspiring.

3D Composition

4D Composition

Three-dimensional composition is just as important as the design of each two-dimensional surface, but unlike surfaces, which usually receive at least *some* attention, the third dimension rarely gets designed unless an architect is involved. This is one of the reasons that architecturally designed homes have a certain something that most people can't put their finger on but really enjoy.

We've looked closely at this home in earlier chapters. From every angle, it is a wonderful three-dimensional composition. The light fixture penetrates through an opening in a freestanding segment of wall and provides lighting for the piano alcove beyond. The eating bar below mimics the

pattern of the light shelf above but stops at the wall segment. Both the eating bar and the light shelf are the same width as the opening in the wall. The segment of wall has been designed as a surface, as has the lower face of the light shelf and the eating bar. But when all three are experienced together they form a very strong three-dimensional composition. Each element relates to the other, either through width, length, or alignment.

In our culture, we tend to design mostly in two dimensions, occasionally in three dimensions, but almost never in four dimensions—taking the dimension of time into account. One of the things I've always loved about Japanese architecture is the integration of the aesthetics of the seasons into the mix. Many homes in Japan have a tokonoma—a small alcove where a poem and an ikebana arrangement (a specially crafted composition of flowers) can be set and changed with the seasons to reflect nature.

There's no reason we can't design a space for the display of seasonally appropriate art in our homes. Architect Cathy Schwabe created a piece of wall art—a series of six identical mini-vases—that the homeowner fills with flowers each week. In consort with the indoor water fountain, this home has a definite sense of the fourth dimension and of our connections with the almost invisible, but ever-present movement of time.

Surface Composition

With an understanding of visual balance, you can make a composition out of very simple forms, as in this music studio. Here, beneath a standard gable roof, the architect has created a very beautiful surface composition out of only three basic elements—a door, a canopy, and a window.

In this architectural version of a haiku, there's greater meaning implied through the use of archetypal forms like the round window; the gentle curve of the canopy; and the basic rectangle of the door, whose glass offers a glimpse within. The only aspect of the design that is purely decorative is the introduction of the three vertical wood strips on the exterior of the circle, which turns the window into its own unique composition.

A much more standard set of parts has been used in an equally simple and creative way by architect Ross Chapin in a small out-building in one of his cottage communities in Washington State. Here the parts are similar, but there is greater attention given to the purely decorative elements—such as the rhythmic batten strips that are painted a lighter hue than the boards whose seams they hide, the six small squares nested between the center battens, and the corner boards and gable frieze board that provide a picture frame for the entire composition. Even though the parts are quite unassuming, the result is visually appealing.

Interruption of Order

When you compose a surface or a three-dimensional composition it's sometimes fun to introduce a form that's not what you'd expect to see. This works especially well when the composition has a strong sense of order to it. So the "odd" element essentially interrupts that order but makes the whole thing more memorable.

In the house shown here, the window to the upper right of the front entry appears to poke through the line of the roof in a very unusual way. It's built like a mini-dormer, but because the trim around the window is a dark color it looks as though only the window protrudes above the roofline. The rest of the house, though exciting to look at with its tower to the left, is still very orderly and predictable. The protruding window makes you take a second look because it interrupts the order.

But remember that a little interruption goes a long way.

Effortlessly Composed

ALL THE HOUSES I've seen by architect Jim Estes and his business partner, Peter Twombly, of Estes/Twombly Architects in Rhode Island, have a real art to their composition, both inside and out. Yet they succeed in accomplishing this with a minimum of means. Their designs are never complicated, never terribly surprising. They employ conventional forms in ways that give the overall composition an effortless

beauty and elegance. You can almost believe their houses have been around forever, fitting in perfectly with their surroundings and with the other houses in the neighborhood.

This unpretentious 2,000-sq.-ft. house for a young couple, one of whom works at home, is a perfect example. It is extraordinary in its simplicity, using only the forms and material combinations typical of the local tradition of shingle-style

A connecting view from the backyard through the middle of the house to the garage beyond introduces us to the engaging three-dimensional composition of this Rhode Island home.

Surface composition. Each material plays a specific role, but none stands out. All work together to make a unified statement.

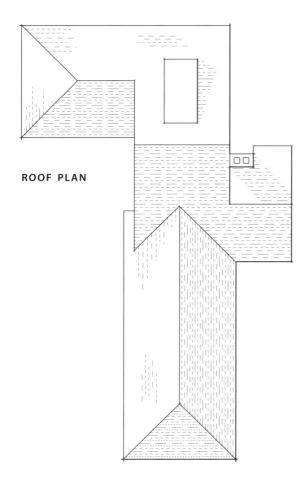

ROOF PLAN

architecture. The house itself is composed of four primary forms: a large gabled-roofed main house, with three "additions" or wings, one gabled and two hipped (though all were in fact built simultaneously, of course). Their shapes effortlessly weave together, each wing projecting from the primary house roof in just the right proportions to emphasize the shape of the main area but retaining a strong character of its own. In combination, the forms produce a very pleasing **three-dimensional composition.**

We discussed the exterior siding treatment for this house several chapters ago as an illustration of Differentiation of Parts and Visual Weight. The differentiation between the lower and the upper segments of the wall, with the lipstick beltline between the two, is an important part of the **surface composition** as well. Every wall of the house has four basic ingredients—beltline, lap siding, shingles, and windows—always applied in the same way.

But there's more to the surface composition than this. Every surface provides a different shape of canvas for the application of the four ingredients. So although they are applied in the same way with respect to each other, the arrangement of windows in relation to the roof shape means that each surface is really a stand-alone composition, as well as a part of a larger whole. Every wall surface you look at has been carefully designed to look balanced from the exterior while simultaneously providing light and view at the appropriate places on the inside. This is one of the secrets of any type of three-dimensional design. The architect or designer doesn't simply compose a shape or a surface for appreciation from one angle alone. Every possible perspective is considered, and he or she adjusts the composition to make it look just right from whatever direction it is viewed.

With a gable-roofed form at the center and two lower-roofed wings stretching from it, the composition has a balanced simplicity that looks effortless—a signature of good design.

CONTRAST

Odd and Even

When a house is composed of pairs of windows, the overall appearance is very different than when the windows are organized in ones and threes. With a pair, the center of the arrangement is the mullion between the two, while with a single window or a series of three, the centerline falls at the middle of the middle window. Although neither arrangement is right or wrong, it is important to observe the differences in the resulting experience.

Sometimes, when a window arrangement provides a focal point for the

house, especially when it aligns with the peak of a gable roof, I prefer to use an odd-numbered configuration so that there is a full piece of glass to look through at the center. To my eye, this feels more satisfying. It emphasizes the unity of the room and of the house it sits in, rather than the duality that is suggested by an equal number of windows flanking a center mullion. The only exception to this is when a pair of French doors falls at the center. In this case, the fact that both doors can be opened to reveal a wider opening, makes it more like a single unit.

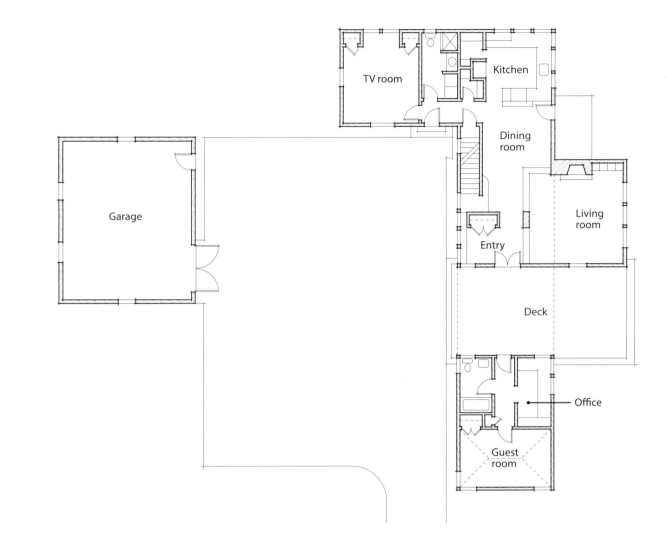

Many of the windows in the wings of the house rest on the beltline that separates lap siding from shingles and are used to help define the corners. By contrast, the windows in the main living space drop below the beltline and are centered on their respective walls.

Now take a look at the **window compositions** and positionings throughout the house. From the exterior, wherever there's a gable, there's an odd-numbered configuration of windows below, so that the center of a window aligns with the peak of the roof ridge. The window composition at the secondary gable-end wall for example—a set of three large double-hungs, with a transom of the same width above the middle one—gives the whole house its focal point and, from within, opens the main living area to the beautiful, wooded surroundings. You can see how the organization of three windows in sequence imparts the sense of unity. The house would look quite different if the set were replaced by an even four-wide configuration. This is really a house that's organized around odd-numbered window combinations, and the introduction of an exception here just wouldn't look right, especially from the outside.

A room with a cathedral ceiling, like this living room, tends to look more balanced if the ridge aligns with the middle of a window, rather than with a dividing mullion.

The only place an even-numbered configuration looks right is at the front door—a pair of French doors that can be thrown open to connect inside and out (see the photo on p. 131). They are centered on the ridge beam above, so when they are closed, there's a sense of duality. But our senses know that they will open to reveal a single opening, so we still understand the underlying unity. However, if there were a central post, as sometimes occurs when two doors are ganged together, the result would be most dissatisfying.

Many architecturally designed homes have a certain something about them that makes you want to linger and soak up their flavor. Although the final design may look effortless and unassuming, the effort that went into making the house look that way was more rigorous than you'd ever imagine.

The chimney to the left of the center window leads our gaze upward, while the door to the deck draws it back down. Together, they create a composition in balance.

TWENTY-FIVE

Expressed Structure

*A house that expresses its structural system on the inside is, for many people,
an attractive alternative to conventional stud-frame construction, in which
the structure is hidden in the walls.*

IF YOU'VE EVER VISITED a house during the construction process, you
know that all the support structure, the beams and columns that transfer
the loads from the roof and the floor platforms down to the ground,
is usually hidden within the walls. But there's another type of house that
expresses its structure in a far more visible way, which is referred to as post
and beam. This is a method of building assembly by which the walls, floor
platforms, and roof are supported by heavy posts (the vertical members) and
beams (the horizontal members), rather than by a multitude of small studs
and rafters as happens in most house construction today.

The frame that is created by this structural system is then enclosed within
an exterior envelope made of any number of materials, from simple plywood to
SIPs—structural insulated panels, which are essentially a plywood sandwich
with rigid insulation in between. Timber framing, the most common type
of post-and-beam construction in use today, uses wooden pegs to secure particular types of wooden joints, including mortise and tenon, dovetails, and scarfs.

The posts and beams provide a form of interior decor that is at once functional, attractive, and informative. It tells the eye how the structure stands up,
while organizing the rooms and spaces between its horizontal and vertical
members. The structure itself creates a visual and three-dimensional ordering system, which is in large part the appeal of this type of home.

But it's still just as important to pay attention
to the proportions of interior space in a post-and-
beam house as it is in one that's conventionally
framed. The house
examples that follow
use their expressed
structure to create both
comfort and character.

Exposed Joists and Rafters

Even in a conventionally built home composed of studs, joists, and rafters, there's the possibility of exposing at least some of the structure. By sheathing the roof with Structural Insulated Panels (SIPs)—essentially a plywood sandwich with rigid insulation in between—or with plywood alone, the supporting rafters can be exposed to the room below. This gives the space a strong sense of order—what we referred to in Chapter 22 as a March. The ceiling surface above the rafters can be painted a contrasting color, as here, or can be left as is, knots and all, for a more organic look.

I've also designed homes in which we've exposed the joists between one level of the house and another, allowing the underside of the floor surface of the upper level to become the ceiling surface for the level below. The house shown above, designed by architect Murray Silverstein, uses this technique to add richness and character to the main level of this simple cottage. It is an inexpensive way to get a wood ceiling, but be aware that sound transmission between levels is significant, since there's only one layer of wood between the two.

Exposed Beams

A popular partial expression of a post-and-beam structure is to expose the beams only. In the home shown here, the architect used heavy, hand-hewn beams instead of the conventional hidden joist system to support the level above, dramatically influencing the character of the room below. If the beams were removed (as shown below), the aesthetic would be lighter and boxier in feel, without the warm intimacy that the dark beams give to the space.

Columns Define Spaces

A column that is placed appropriately to define one area of the house from another while simultaneously providing its supporting function can be a wonderful enhancement to a living space.

In the delightful rambler remodel shown here there used to be a solid wall between the kitchen and the dining area. The new openness between the two was made possible by introducing a series of posts and beams, which also provide the infrastructure for a whimsical canvas ceiling that gives the entire area a soft, mellifluous character. The columns subtly differentiate the kitchen from the dining area without obstructing sight lines.

If you think back to Chapter 2, Shelter around Activity, you'll see that the columns here, in combination with the lowered ceiling over the kitchen, distinctly define and shelter the kitchen from the dining area, making a living area that is more a Sequence of Places than a single undifferentiated great room or a series of discrete, separate rooms. In general, columns usually add rather than subtract character.

Brackets

A bracket is a piece of wood or metal that is used to transfer loads from a horizontal or sloped structural member to a vertical member below. Brackets were frequently used to add character to the exterior of the bungalows of the early part of the twentieth century. Today, with our dependence on truss technology and shallower overhangs, brackets are used only rarely. But even when their design is kept simple, as shown above, they add a lot to the personality of a home.

Brackets can be used internally as well, as in a true timber-frame home. They are often carved and decorated to add some character to a room.

Artful Structure

The structural components of a building can be artful expressions in their own right. This requires that the same skills of composition we discussed in the previous chapter be brought to bear on the relationships among structural components.

In the room shown above, the roof of this basic cabin is supported by standard rafters, but instead of spacing them evenly across the ceiling plane as is normally done, here they've been doubled up, with a $1\frac{1}{2}$-in. space between the two. Every other doubled rafter pair then provides a pocket for a horizontal wood tie, which spans the building, creating a simple truss. The structural elements lend a modest elegance to the space below.

Structural Quality

This home bears a strong resemblance to the heavy timber construction of a traditional Japanese farmhouse, but it has been tailored to fit a contemporary Western lifestyle.

PEOPLE WHO HIRE an architect to help with the design of a home often arrive with a definite set of aesthetic preferences and lifestyle goals. Such was the case with the client for the new home shown here. The owner, an educator and writer by trade, was a lover of Japanese aesthetics and everyday rituals. He hired architect Hiroshi Morimoto because of his ability to translate these for a Westerner into a design that could bridge both cultures.

While the structural system is reminiscent of traditional Japanese farmhouses of old, the spaces within have been crafted into a Sequence of Places for a contemporary Western lifestyle. At the same time, the beauty of the structural wood members, the way that each beam, column, and rafter is connected to adjacent structural members, and the resulting shapes of spaces created provide the primary aesthetic for the home. This is a wonderful example of an expressed

A long skylight at the ridge of the main roof floods the center of the house with light, casting ever-changing shadow patterns across the surfaces of the beams and columns as the sun moves across the sky.

heavy timber "skeleton" that provides an infrastructure for a design that truly enhances the quality of life within its boundaries.

Traditional farmhouses in Japan were made with large, dark-stained timbers, and their interiors, though vaulting and airy in scale, were also dark and mysterious because of a lack of light from above. Morimoto used similar sizes of beams and columns, and an equally visible roof form, but added a skylight at the ridge of the roof that floods the main living area with daylight. Because the structural members are left their natural color, the home has a much more contemporary feel, even though the forms are classic.

One of the aspects of Japanese timber-frame design that I find particularly appealing is the use of deep beams that run across the width of the structure. If you look closely, you'll see that in this house there are in fact **exposed beams** running in both directions, those in the north-south

Typical of traditional Japanese carpentry, the roof structure of beams and rafters is exposed, giving each room a distinctive personality. The lower portions of the roof have twice as many rafters as the portions above the beams, establishing a pleasing rhythm.

direction resting atop the ones that run east-west (see the photo on the facing page). In combination, these beams define an implied ceiling that helps bring the height of the space down to human scale, making the room below more comfortable to sit in and more intimate, in spite of its size. Remove the beams, however, and the space would feel overwhelming unless there were a lot of people in the room. The beams help create a sense of Shelter around Activity.

Even in some of the less focal spaces, the heavy timber structure lends character and form to the activity areas below. For example, the expressed gabled roof structure makes the in-home office and writing studio shown on p. 225 into an independent mini-house within the larger house. And throughout the home, the roof form plays an important role in adding both charm and detail to the rooms, walkways, and interior views. No matter where you look, the structural members tell the eye how the house is supported

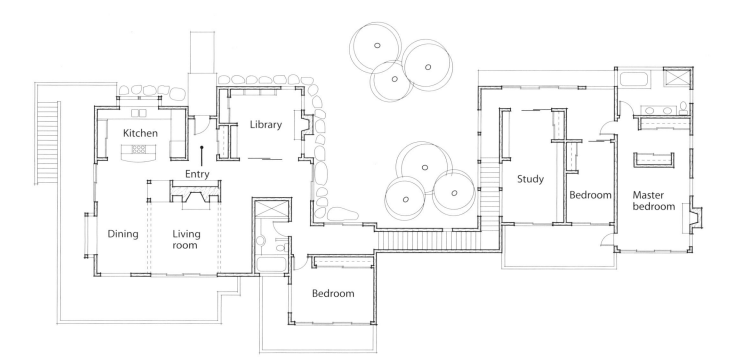

and simultaneously lend a natural beauty and spatial hierarchy to every area.

The attention to detail continues all the way to the micro level, with every joint and connection in the building made as a work of art. This is one of the reasons that Japanese aesthetics have the ability to move people so. It's not just the "look" that we are responding to, but the fact that every stroke of the carpenter's tools has been performed with a deep sense of caring and presence. Although we have no words for the quality of experience that results from this level of craft, anyone who has experienced architecture made in this way will readily attest to its power and ability to delight. There are things beyond the visible that affect us deeply. Much of the time, we're simply not aware this is so.

A number of beams run the full length of the main house, leading our gaze to the windows at the far end and to the garden beyond. These long views through give a clear sense of the artful structure that makes a timber-frame house so attractive.

IN PUBLIC

Parque Guell

Catalan architect Antonio Gaudi (1852-1926) is famous for the way he "expressed" the structural systems of his whimsical buildings. He would first build an elaborate inverted model using wires, from which he then hung weights proportional to the load that each structural member would have to carry. The shape that each wire took as a result defined the shape for that particular wall or column in its full-scale, right-way-up version. Here, at Parque Guell in Barcelona, Spain, the columns supporting the plaza above are leaning inward—the perfect angle to most efficiently transfer the loads from above into the earth below.

TWENTY-SIX

Point of Focus

*Many rooms and spaces benefit greatly from the creation of a focal point
to attract attention and give significance to a particular area.*

A POINT OF FOCUS can be as simple as a favorite piece of art at the center of the main living space. Or it can be more elaborate, like an inglenook around a beautifully designed fireplace or a composition of windows looking into the garden beyond. Although it's not crucial to have a point of focus in every space in the house, the introduction of one or two in key rooms can add a lot of character. These focal points act in a similar way as the source of light in the principle, Light to Walk Toward. Whether the focus is a painting, a window seat, or a striking piece of furniture or built-in, its purpose is to draw you into the space and to give the area a center.

When remodeling a house and money is limited, one of my favorite strategies to add character is to create a Point of Focus in the kitchen on the wall area between the range and the hood above. The hood is almost always located higher above the countertop than the adjacent cabinets, so it creates a natural focus in the backsplash area, even without further embellishment. But by filling this area with a tile design, you can simply and inexpensively add a point of focus that will be seen and enjoyed every day. In the remodeling of my own home in North Carolina, I used a single feature tile at the center of the area above the cooktop and surrounded it with much less expensive tile (see the photo in "Focus at the End of an Axis" on p. 230). Because the range is located at the approximate center of the visual axis from the main living area to the kitchen, it is seen many times a day and adds some personality to a space that would otherwise be unremarkable.

When you apply this principle in your own home you can be as creative as you like, using objects that have meaning to you.

Focal Wall Surface

In many rooms, there is an obvious focal wall surface. Usually it's focal because of one of the following: It is directly above a fireplace or built-in TV; it is bathed in light from a skylight or adjacent window, making it more noticeable; it is the tallest wall in the room, perhaps beneath the ridge of a cathedral ceiling; or it is at the far end of a strong visual axis through the house.

The wall shown here is focal for all four of these reasons, making it even more of a Point of Focus than usual. The wall hanging has been placed directly above the fireplace and is washed with light from the large skylight above. The hanging could have been placed at the center of the wall, but since the fireplace is off to the left of center, as is the skylight, this might have made the room appear lopsided. By hanging it on the same side of the wall as the fireplace and the skylight, the owner is emphasizing that this is really the center of the room.

Room Focus

Sometimes you'll want to create a Focal Point for a room that defines its center and draws the attention in that direction. This can be done with a window composition, or it can be something like a fireplace or a TV that commands attention because of its function.

I employed this strategy several years ago when designing this home. The family acknowledged that, though they loved the look of a fireplace, they seldom gathered around it. Their primary social gathering place was in front of the TV screen. So we designed a set of cabinets around the TV to create an interesting visual composition as the focus of the room. The fireplace is located off to one side, where it provides a Point of Focus at the end of the main walkway through the house. Both the TV and the fireplace, then, are points of focus, but the TV is the Room Focus, while the fireplace is a Focus at the End of an Axis.

Focus at the End of an Axis

In most houses there is usually at least one long visual axis through the space, and sometimes many more. By this I mean that you can see through one space after another to a wall or window at the far end of the vista. When such a vista exists, the end wall surface is given increased importance. It automatically becomes one of those places that cries out for a piece of artwork—or some other object or feature — that will provide a striking visual delight. Your attention is directed there anyway, so why not make the most of it?

In my own kitchen, the wall above the cooktop is at the center of the visual axis as you enter the room from the adjacent living space. The single handmade tile surrounded by standard tiles captures the attention. Without the tile design, the wall would seem naked and in need of a focal point.

Something Place

One of my favorite techniques when designing a new home or remodel is to include a few "something places." These are natural Points of Focus that can be enhanced, either through special lighting or through sculpting of the available space, to accentuate the area in question and make it suitable for exhibiting a piece of artwork or special treasure.

The Something Place shown here is in one of the corners of an upstairs landing, created by the octagonal ceiling above. Because this particular spot is passed by every time someone heads from any one of the bedrooms to the stairway, it has a natural importance to it.

This Something Place has been crafted to feature what it contains. The ceiling is lowered over the area to the height of the headband, providing a perfect spot for a small recessed light to pinpoint the object below. At night the lamp's reflection off the sculpture also provides a soft illumination for the entire landing area, while simultaneously adding drama and character.

Attention Grabber

Another, more dramatic way to create a Point of Focus is to make an unusual piece of craftsmanship the primary attention grabber for a room, or even for the entire house, as in the home shown above. This amazing stone chimney, crafted by stone mason Jeff Gamelin in a house on the coast of Maine designed by architect Robert Knight, is a wonderful example of a piece of construction that transcends its normal utilitarian function and becomes perhaps the most memorable feature of the entire house. (There's also a tiny Something Place built right into the chimney to display a treasured shell.)

An attention grabber doesn't have to be a visual feature. It can also be directed at a different sense, like the water feature in the entryway of the home shown above, whose sound permeates both levels. No matter where you are in the house, you are drawn toward the feature's calming brook-like sound, giving the home a strong sense of "center" and tranquility. Although the surrounding architecture makes a strong statement, it's the water feature that makes it an attention grabber.

Multiple Focus

On the approach to this Rhode Island cottage, the "attention grabber" is the prominent tower, which has a panoramic overlook of the surroundings.

The unusual dormer that interrupts the roofline is a secondary attention grabber on the front of the house.

ARCHITECT JIM ESTES is a master at allowing a house to reveal itself through its various Points of Focus in a way that both delights and charms the visitor into feeling completely at home. None of the Points of Focus he uses is in the least flamboyant, and none is contrived. Each is perfectly integrated into the whole, completely at ease in its surroundings, yet powerfully apparent as the key place or object in its space.

As you drive up to this little Rhode Island cottage, your attention is immediately grabbed by the tower to the left-hand side of the building—a lookout that echoes the form of a small square lighthouse just a mile south of this home. A secondary **attention grabber** (as we discussed in Chapter 24) is the small window dormer that pokes up above the sloped roof plane. It's a surprise—not something you'd expect to see in a house composed of such familiar forms—and so we take notice of it in passing. And then, of course, there's the most obvious Point of Focus, the front door, which falls directly below the central window at the gabled peak of the roof, which

in turn is in the middle of the composition of the entire house. So right from the get-go, the visitor to the house is engaged in the home's drama and playfulness.

Whether you enter from the side of the house or the front, you are led into the main living area, whose focal object is the fireplace opener), set at

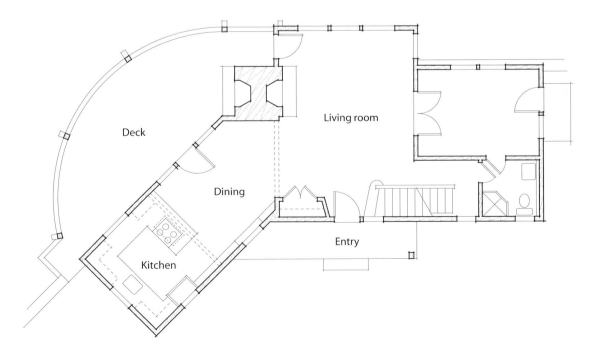

Deck

Living room

Dining

Entry

Kitchen

In the kitchen, the cooktop hood is a strong Point of Focus and its graceful lines echo the curve of the ceiling.

The window at the far end of the kitchen is a focus at the end of the main axis, which helps draw us into the space. Above the island, the cooktop hood creates a visual bridge between kitchen and dining area.

the approximate center of the wall separating living and dining areas and, more important, at the pivot point between the two rectangular forms that constitute the floor plan (see the photo on p. 228). Not only is the fireplace made of natural materials, in contrast to the surrounding painted surfaces, but it is also significantly darker in color, giving it Visual Weight, with a striking stone lintel (the piece above the fireplace opening) that is much more organic in form than the rest of the stone. So the eye is left with no doubt that this is the **room focus.**

As you continue into the house, through the framed opening that defines the entry into the dining area, your attention is redirected to the far end of the space to an alcove containing the kitchen. Your gaze comes to rest on the beautiful form of the cooktop hood, a sculptural marriage of glass and stainless steel that serves both a functional and an aesthetic role in the design. Because there is a strong light source behind it, you are drawn toward it. But instead of the window becoming the Point of Focus, the hood, which is loosely aligned with it, takes center stage. The light behind the object silhouettes its unusual form, making it the focus of the room. This is a clever trick. It is often difficult to make something in the middle of a space the Point of Focus, unless there is a significant amount of feature lighting directed at it. By using the window to strengthen the hood, it has been made into an attention grabber (because of its shape), a **something place** (because of the window's silhouetting), and a **focus at the end of an axis.**

There are two more Points of Focus in the room, one that we can see in the photographs and one that we must look to the floor plan to understand. The one we can see is the door to the porch, which, when opened as here, attracts attention to itself because of its darker color, giving it the

The dark green of the door to the deck creates a strong color contrast with the bright white of the interior trim.

Visual Weight that makes it the most noticeable object in view (see the photo above). The dining table is centered on the doorway, as seems logical. The less obvious Point of Focus is the center of the table itself, which is in fact the center point of the curved deck and trellis beyond the doorway (see the plan on p. 233).

This is the kind of focal point that may not be consciously observable but that gives the house its sense of integrity. Architects will make use of these kinds of alignments and hidden compositional keys all the time. I don't know that even we fully appreciate how powerful their effects can be upon the experiencing of a space, but in plan, as well as from the perspective of the dining room and the deck beyond, you have a sense of its importance.

Outdoor spaces also benefit from Points of Focus. This curving deck has two: by day, the panoramic ocean view, and in the evening, an outside fireplace.

TWENTY-SEVEN

Organizing Strategy

*The way that a house is organized can be thought of as the conceptual form
behind the physical shapes that we see with our eyes and experience
with our senses.*

WHEN YOU LOOK AT THE FLOOR PLAN of a house, your focus
will typically gravitate to the adjacencies of one room to another.
You may be interested to see how closely the floor plan would fit
your own lifestyle. Or you may be looking for unusual features that could give
you some ideas for different ways of arranging the rooms of your own home.
But it is rare that you'll look beyond these kinds of specifics to the Organizing
Strategy for the house as a whole.

Is it a house with the main living spaces all arranged in a simple square floor
plan, for example; or is it a long, narrow house that lets in lots of light on both
sides of every room? Is it a grouping of small buildings rather than a single
structure, or is it a series of wings arranged around a courtyard? All these
approaches to organizing a house plan produce very different characters of
home, and understanding their implications and potentials is just as important
a decision in the design process as determining the relationships among rooms.
When a house has no organizing strategy it has no sense of integrity, and often
appears haphazard and random.

Some architects have favorite Organizing Strategies that you'll see time and
again in the houses they design, if you know what to look for. Frank Lloyd
Wright is famous for organizing his houses around a central fireplace, for
example. There are literally hundreds of ways to organize a house, and it's
impossible to innumerate them all here, but in this chapter we'll look at
some of the most common ones, to help you rec-
ognize the defining characteristics of each, along
with their pros, their
cons, and their cost
implications.

Simple Square or Rectangle

The simplest and least expensive way to organize a house is to keep the foundation and main floor plan square or rectangular. By restricting the exterior corners of the footprint to the logical minimum, the structure is easy to build and so tends to cost less than one with more "bumps" in and out. The house shown here is a simple rectangle with two bumpouts, one in the bathroom and one for the living room window seat. Both bumpouts are cantilevered so the foundation below has no jogs in it, to keep costs down.

The organizing strategy here is one of keeping all the rooms and spaces very simple in form, with sliding partitions and a minimum number of fixed walls added to define one place from another. When money is tight, this is by far the best approach for controlling costs. It also allows you to add special details later if desired, rather than make them a necessary part of the infrastructure of the house. If, in addition, the second floor is stacked directly above the first and the roof is kept as a simple gable, costs for the container of the interior space—what architects refer to as the building envelope—will be kept in check.

Bedroom　　Living　　　　　　Dining

Long Thin House

This is a variant of the simple rectangle that is particularly attractive because it allows every room to have light from at least two sides. The house shown here— a truly tiny house that's only 10 ft. wide but 60 ft. long — is bright and visually appealing, giving an immediate sense of spaciousness as a result. Light enters the space from both the front and the back of every room, and even though the structure is narrow, because you can see from one end of the house to the other through the open doors on the same side of every room in the house, there's a very long interior view that belies its overall size.

Circulation Spine

Master bedroom wing

Living space

Garage

Circulation spine

Guest bedroom wing

A favorite organizing strategy for many architects is to lay out the rooms of the house along a circulation spine—a long walkway connecting one end of the house to the other. Rooms and spaces can either open off one side only ("single-loaded") or off both sides ("double-loaded"). We're familiar with this organizing strategy in many other types of buildings. Think of most of the hotels you've visited and you'll realize that the hotel rooms are usually distributed along either side of a long hallway. In many ways, a circulation spine functions the same way as the spine in a human body, allowing energy and signals of the nervous system to be moved up and down the system as necessary.

This southwestern house is organized around a circulation spine that is mostly single loaded, except at the guest bedroom wing, where it turns into a double-loaded corridor, with guest bedrooms opening off one side and the dining room and kitchen opening off the other. The architect uses the lowered ceiling height of the hallway to define the spine, rather than always enclosing it with solid walls. But at the two ends of the long spine, the hallway becomes more enclosed, giving a strong sense of boundary and containment.

Around a Courtyard

Another organizing strategy that appeals to many people is to distribute the rooms of the house around a courtyard. However, it is an expensive option because you almost double the surface area of the exterior walls of the house and significantly complicate the foundation when you have an exterior open space at the center.

In hot dry climates, interior courtyards have some significant benefits in terms of comfort in addition to their aesthetic charm. With its large fish pond and abundant vegetation, the courtyard shown here provides a cooling effect for the house. With windows and doors opened to the courtyard, the home's interior feels cooler. The surrounding covered walkway also provides a cool and beautiful circulation space.

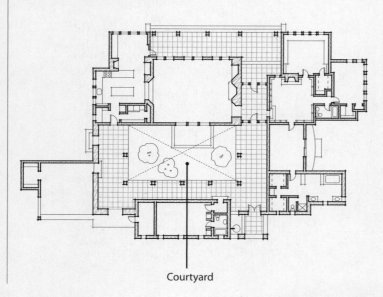

Courtyard

Assemblage of Structures

If money is not a big issue and you want your home to feel more like a village than a single house, you can build a series of structures, each with its own separate walls and roof. This organizing strategy is the most expensive option because the amount of wall, roof, and foundation area are all increased, while the volume of space enclosed remains the same.

In this home, architect Scott Smith used simple materials and forms to keep the costs of the added surface area to a minimum. The result, is a loose but charming interrelationship between the different structures, just like a small village.

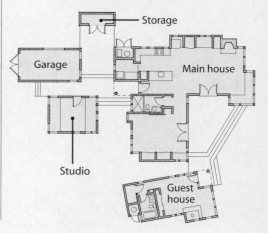

Storage

Garage

Main house

Studio

Guest house

Simple, but Elegant

T HIS SIMPLE POST-AND-BEAM home is a beautiful example of a **long thin house** that expresses its structural system on the interior, and in so doing provides definition and Visual Weight for each of the main-level living spaces. The primary rectangle in plan is 24 ft. wide—the width of the two-car garage—and 54 ft. long and is roofed with a basic gable that extends the length of the house. The entire distance of the house from end to end is 62 ft. 6 in.,

The views through this house emphasize its organizational strategy. It is immediately recognizable as a long thin house, with light entering the main living space from three sides, a march of beams and columns defining one room from the next, and a strong central alignment.

Though there are no solid walls along this arcade, there's no doubt that it is a hallway. The columns and beams on either side provide the definition.

with the living room and master bedroom above sticking out an additional 12 ft. beyond.

Whether arriving from the street or from the alley at the back of the house, guests are welcomed into the home via the same linear path that runs the length of the structure. There's nothing about this house that seems complicated or abstract, yet the diversity of character of space has been attained by the clever use of a simple and elegant structural system. The posts and beams help us understand the relationships between rooms, and spaces, and the house as a whole.

If you look at the organization of the main rectangle in the plan on p. 244, you'll see that the post-and-beam section is the same width as the living room bumpout—17 ft.—and extends into the main 24-ft.-wide rectangle. So the architects, while starting with the concept of a long thin house, actually organized the plan around the interpenetration of two long thin rectangles, as you can see in the floor plan. The same interpenetration occurs on the upper level, and you can readily see the same defining lines between the smaller and larger rectangles.

Architects will often use an Organizing Strategy such as this, with the same pattern of structure and wall positioning on both levels. Even though the alignments of the overlapping rectangles may not be consciously perceived by visitors to the home, at a subliminal level most architects believe that such ordering principles make a difference to our experience of space.

A long thin house often belies its actual square footage. From the path adjacent to the garage you can see the full length of the structure, which makes it look significantly larger than it really is.

A post-and-beam structural system adds a lot of character to the spaces it supports and defines. It also lends a quality of permanence that is at once attractive and functional.

At the front of the house, guests are greeted by an intimate stone terrace, which opens off the living area.

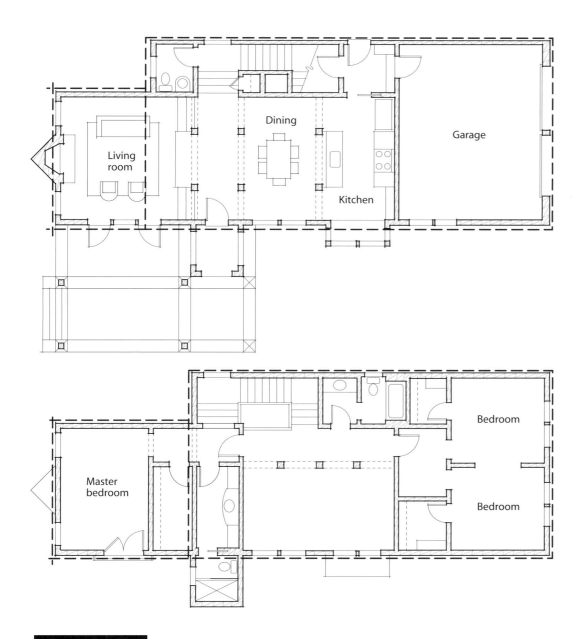

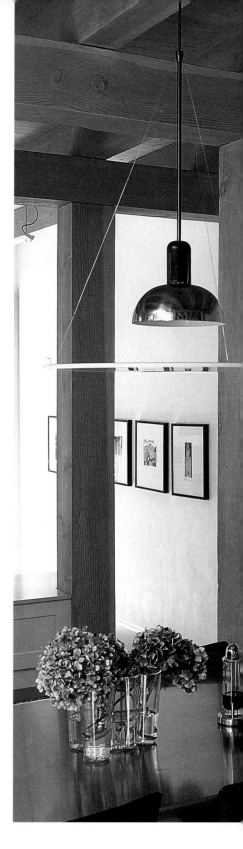

Choosing a Strategy

In developing a plan for a new home, an architect typically starts to formulate a design direction by selecting an Organizational Strategy. After listening carefully to his or her clients' wishes, and after studying the site on which the house will be placed, the architect usually starts the design process by generating a number of schematics—drawings that suggest different ways of organizing the house and laying out the rooms and spaces therein.

If the budget is tight, the organizing strategy selected will be one that minimizes surface area for the volume contained and keeps the construction methods as straightforward as possible. A simple square or rectangle with a basic gable roof would be a good choice when funds are limited. But when money is not such a constraint, a house with more complexity of form and greater surface area is possible. In this case, the option of organizing the plan around a central courtyard or of creating a house with several wings of rooms might be considered. There are more corners, and there's more surface area for the volume and square footage contained within the building "envelope."

No one strategy is better or worse, but each gives a different underlying character to the resulting home.

Though the layout of the house is highly organized, the wood of the heavy timbers lends a natural warmth to the living spaces.

The expressed structure of the main living area stands in contrast to the simple unadorned forms and white walls of the rest of the house. It's the contrast between the two that gives the house its strength of character.

In three dimensions, the living room/dining room/kitchen rectangle is very obvious. The heavy timber posts and beams divide one space from the next, creating a wonderful sense of layering, as well as defining the main entry into the house and the pathway through the house to the stairway across from the front door. There are no interior walls, just a series of columns—framed openings if you will—that delineate the extent of each activity area. In the photo on p. 241, you can see from the dining table through the entry walkway to the fireplace on the far wall beyond. Looking back through the space from the living room (above), the same configuration of activity areas is clear, but this time the kitchen cooktop and hood provide the central Point of Focus, instead of the fireplace. The Sequence of Places is so unassuming, so effortless, and yet so delightful precisely because of its simplicity.

IN MANY WAYS, architects are masters of illusion. They can make a little space look like a lot. They can make structures of brick or stone appear to defy gravity. And they can turn something of apparent insignificance into an experience with the power to move us deeply. But it's not magic. As we've seen, the architect's craft has certain underlying principles that anyone can understand. Now that you have the knowledge to apply some of the same things in your own home, you may be wondering where to start. Although each principle is relatively simple, integrating them into a house can be a challenge.

If you were to apply every idea in this book, the result might well be overwhelming. Just as with composing a sentence, there's a fine line between artful crafting and too much complexity. Comprehensibility is lost as the length and complexity of the sentence structure increase. So unless your design challenge is a simple one, it's a good idea to hire an architect or an interior designer to help you integrate the principles into your house.

Many people are afraid to do this, though, thinking that the person they hire won't understand what they want. Because most of us live in houses all our lives, we assume we know how to design one. But as you've seen in the preceding pages, there's a lot more to it than meets the eye, and knowing how to make a house that's both beautiful and functional takes some practice. Architects are trained to work *with* you, to listen to what you want, and to help you find a solution that really meets your needs. You can find appropriate professionals to help you on my website, www.sarahsusanka.com, or by calling your local chapter of the American Institute of Architects (AIA) or the American Society of Interior Designers (ASID).

There are thousands of houses built every year in the production home market that have little input from the homeowner until they are ready for sale. These houses provide adequate shelter and function, but they could do so much more than that. Here again, there's a place for a new type of house design—a greater collaboration between architect and developer—to bring to market some designs that are less constrained by the "dollars per square foot" mentality and more focused on quality and character of the house, both inside and out.

My hopes in writing this book are that by introducing you to the tools in the architect's toolbox, there will be a new way for homeowners, builders, designers, and architects to communicate with one another about home. And that by revealing the hidden dimensions of spatial experience that lie beneath the surface style, everyone involved in the designs of our homes will become familiar with and start applying these principles to create better, more inspiring living space.

A house composed using these principles—a home by design—is far more than just a place to live. If you've ever had the opportunity to visit such a home, you'll know that it engages you in a sort of experiential dance from the moment you step inside to the moment you leave. It's literally as though the house has its own life force, its own vitality. And if you are lucky enough to live in a home by design, you know that it affects the quality of your life in a profound way, infusing the ordinary rituals of everyday life with delight and inspiration.

What you'll discover as you apply these principles in your own house is that we are vastly more affected by spatial experience than we typically realize. Equipped with the words to describe these experiences, you can now replicate them in your own house to transform it into a place that really feels like home—by design, of course.

WILLIAM ADAMS ARCHITECTS
450 San Juan Avenue
Venice, California 90291
(310) 458-9397
www.wadamsarchitects.com

Principal Architect(s): Bill Adams, Carl Smith

Page(s): 39 (top middle, top right), 64 (top left), 71 (bottom middle), 74, 78–81, 118 (top left), 124, 153 (top right, bottom right)

BERNIE BAKER
Bernie Baker Architect, P.S.
5571 Welfare Ave., NE
Bainbridge Island, WA 98110
(206) 842-6278
bba@bainbridge.net

Principal Architect: Bernie Baker, P.S.

Page: 85 (upper left)

CANTILEVER STUDIOS
1270 Cleveland Avenue #216
San Diego, California 92103
(619) 948-1544
www.cantileverstudios.com

Principal Architect: Christina Code Mannion, AIA, NCARB

Page(s): 163–165, 168 (top left)

CENTERBROOK ARCHITECTS & PLANNERS
67 Main Street
P.O. Box 955
Centerbrook, Connecticut 06409
(860) 767-0175
www.centerbrook.com

Principal Architect(s): House: James C. Childress, FAIA
Music Studio: James C. Childress, FAIA with Stephen B. Holmes
Builder: Triangle Builders

Page(s): 3 (bottom right), 23 (bottom middle), 129 (bottom right), 195, 198–201, 204 (bottom right), 214 (top left), 223 (top right)

CHAMBERS & CHAMBERS
68 Sycamore Avenue
Mill Valley, California 94941
(415) 381-8326

Principal Architect: Barbara Chambers

Page(s): 2, 23 (bottom middle), 8 (top left, top middle, top right), 18, 60, 115 (bottom right), 158, 176, 236, 241–245

ROSS CHAPIN ARCHITECTS
P.O. Box 230
Langley, Washington 98260
(360) 221-2373
www.rosschapin.com

Principal Architect(s): Ross Chapin AIA, John Prietto, Eric Richmond, Matthew Swett
Developer/Contractor: The Cottage Company, LLC
Interior Designer: Ross Chapin, AIA

Page(s): 23 (top right), 62 (bottom left), 63 (bottom left), 77 (top right), 82, 108 (bottom middle), 119 (top middle),180 (top left), 196 (top right), 214 (bottom middle), 223 (bottom middle)

CUNNINGHAM & QUILL ARCHITECTS, PLLC
1054 31st Street, NW
Suite 315
Washington, DC 20007
(202) 337-0090
www.cunninghamquill.com

Principal Architect: Ralph Cunningham, AIA

Page(s): 54 (top left), 65–67, 92 (top right, bottom right), 169 (top left, bottom right), 188 (top left)

ESTES/TWOMBLY ARCHITECTS, INC.
79 Thames Street
Newport, Rhode Island
(401) 846-3336
www.estestwombly.com

Principal Architect: James Estes
Builder: Bruce Moniz, BAM Building Corporation

Page(s): 7 (top right), 31 (top right), 108 (top right), 144 (top right), 180 (top right), 214 (top right), 228, 232–235

Principal Architect: James Estes; Builder: Allan Randall
Page(s): 38 (top right), 52, 76 (bottom right), 108 (top left), 162 (top right, bottom right), 190 (top right), 215–219

Page(s): 54 (top right), 76 (top left)

GARY FURMAN ARCHITECTS
708 Rio Grande Street
Austin, Texas 78701
(512) 479-4100
www.garyfurmanarchitects.com

Architect Team: Gary Furman, Patrick Alexander
Builder: Schatz Homes

Page(s): 71 (top left), 98, 102–105, 109 (top right), 146 (bottom middle, bottom right), 206 (top middle), 240 (top left)

Principal Architect(s): Gary Furman, Philip Keil
Builder: Ariston Homes
Interior Designer: Ed Martens and Ariston Homes

Page(s): 22 (top right), 23 (top left), 68, 210

Principal Architect(s): Gary Furman, Patrick Alexander
Builder: Dalgleish Construction

Interior Designer: Clayton Morgan Design

Page(s): 30 (top left), 36, 39 (top left), 55 (top left), 101 (top left, bottom left), 117, 136 (top left), 186, 188 (top right), 204 (top left, top right)

GOULD EVANS
4041 Mill Street
Kansas City, Missouri 64111
(816) 931-6655
www.gouldevans.com

Principal Architect(s): Bob Gould, Neal Angrisano, Rohn Grotenhuis, Jon Birke
Interior Designer: Karen Gould

Page(s): 55 (top right), 70 (top left, bottom left), 110 (top right, middle right), 121–123, 136, 127 (top right), 136 (top right), 181 (top left), 197 (top left)

ROBIN GRAY ARCHITECTS, LLC
511 Agua Fria
Santa Fe, New Mexico 87501
(505) 995-8411
www.robingray.net

Principal Architect: Robin Gray
Builder: Compadre Custom Construction

Page(s): 7 (top left), 47 (bottom middle, bottom right), 54 (top middle), 120 (top left), 128 (top left), 134, 138–141, 239 (top left, bottom middle)

HUESTIS TUCKER ARCHITECTS, LLC
2349 Whitney Avenue
Hamden, Connecticut 06518
(203) 248-1007
www.huestistucker.com

Principal Architect(s): Jennifer Huestis, Robert Tucker
Builder: Canedo Brothers Builders

Page(s): Cover, 24–27, 30 (top right, bottom middle), 62 (top left, top right), 84 (top left), 92 (top left), 161 (top right, bottom right), 168 (bottom right), 197 (top middle)

JACOBSON SILVERSTEIN WINSLOW ARCHITECTS
3106 Shattuck Ave.
Berkeley, CA 94705
(510) 848-8861
www.jswarch.com

Principal Architect(s): Max Jacobson, Murray Silverstein, Barbara Winslow

Page(s): 37 (middle bottom), 38 (top and bottom left), 61 (middle bottom), 107 (middle bottom)

KARREMAN & ASSOCIATES
231 Gowen Place, NW
Bainbridge Island, Washington 98110
(206) 842-1253
www.karreman.com

Principal Architect: Frank Karreman
Builder: Seahome Services, Inc.

Page(s): 23 (top middle), 27 (bottom right), 46 (top left), 63 (top left), 152 (top right), 153 (top left, bottom left), 180 (bottom middle), 181 top middle, top right), 196 (top middle), 223 (top middle)

KAWELL MOONEYSAWYER
ARCHITECTS & BUILDERS
6425 City West Parkway
Eden Prairie, Minnesota 55344
(952) 942-9982
www.kawell.com

Principal Architect: Mark A. Kawell, AIA
Builder: Kawell Mooney Sawyer
Interior Designer: JK Interiors

Page(s): 48–51, 147–149, 190–192

ROBERT KNIGHT, AIA
Knight Associates
P.O. Box 803
Blue Hill, ME 04610
(207) 374-2761
www.knightarchitect.com

Principal Architect: Robert Knight, AIA

Page(s): 223, 231

KODET ARCHITECTURAL GROUP, LTD.
15 Groveland Terrace
Minneapolis, MN 55403
(612) 377-2737

Principal Architect: Ed Kodet, FAIA

Page(s): 130 (middle right)

MORGANTE WILSON ARCHITECTS, LTD.
3813 North Ravenswood
Chicago, Illinois 60613
(773) 528-1001
www.morgantewilson.com

Principal Architect(s): Elissa Morgante, Fred Wilson
Interior Designers: Elissa Morgante, Fred Wilson

Page(s): 31 (top middle), 47 (top middle), 118 (top right), 119 (top left), 137 (bottom right), 178, 182–185

MORIMOTO ARCHITECTS
1200 Tenth Street
Berkeley, California 94710
(510) 527-8800
www.morimotoarch.com

Principal Architect: Hiroshi Morimoto
Interior Designer: Virginia D. Wilson Interiors

Page(s): 72–73, 92 (top middle), 193 (top right, middle right), 220, 224–227

Principal Architect: Hiroshi Morimoto
Contractor: Alderson Construction

Page(s): Acknowledgments (top left), 9 (bottom left), 63 (top right), 76 (top right), 77 (top middle), 93 (top middle, top right), 145 (bottom right), 170–175, 181 (bottom right), 200 (bottom right), 205

FIONA E. O'NEILL, ARCHITECT
1000 Annapolis Road
The Sea Ranch, California 95497-0108
(707) 785-0040
fionaone@mcn.org

Principal Architect: Fiona E. O'Neill
Builder: Sea Ranch Ventures, Inc.

Page(s): 64 (top right, bottom right), 70 (top right),90, 94–97, 100 (top left, top right), 238 (top left)

SALA ARCHITECTS, INC.
43 Main Street, SE, Suite 410
Minneapolis, Minnesota 55414
(612) 379-3037
www.SALAarc.com

Principal Architect(s): Eric Odor, Bryan Anderson
Builder: Schwalbe Construction, Inc.

Page(s): 56–59, 71 (top right), 84 (top right), 110 (top left), 129 (top middle, top right), 144 (top left), 145 (top right), 160 (top left), 190 (top left), 206 (top right), 213 (top left, top middle)

Principal Architect(s): Eric Odor, Sarah Susanka
Builder: Erotas Building Corporation
Interior Designer(s): Deb Emert of E Design

Page(s): 44, 111–115, 118 (bottom middle), 119 (top right), 169 (bottom right), 189 (top left), 212 (top right)

SALA ARCHITECTS, INC./
STILLWATER BRANCH
904 South Fourth St.
Stillwater, MN 55082
(651) 351-0961
www.SALAarc.com

Principal Architect(s): Kelly R. Davis AIA with Timothy Old
Builder: Andlar Construction, Inc.

Page(s): 31 (top left), 40–43, 47 (top left, top right), 55 (bottom middle), 129 (top left), 146 (top left), 153 (top middle), 212 (top left, top middle), 230 (top left)

CATHY SCHWABE ARCHITECTURE
470 49th Street
Oakland, California 94609
(510) 658-3651

Principal Architect(s): Cathy Schwabe with EHDD Architecture
Builder: Drew Maran Construction
Interior Designer(s): Sandra Slater with Fu Tung Cheng

Page(s): 144 (top middle), 145 (top left), 202, 207–209, 213 (top right), 231 (top right)

SARAH SUSANKA, AIA
www.sarahsusanka.com

Principal Architect(s): Sarah Susanka with Paul Hannan. Project completed while at Mulfinger, Susanka, Mahady & Partners (now SALA Architects)
Builder: Architects Plus
Interior Colorist: Susan Moore

Page(s): 10–17, 46 (top middle), 101 (top right, bottom right), 109 (top left), 152 (top left), 168 (bottom left), 217 (bottom left, middle right), 230 (top middle), 231 (top left)

Principal Architect: Sarah Susanka

Page(s): 162 (top left), 230 (top middle, top right)

TEA2 ARCHITECTS
2724 West 43rd Street
Minneapolis, Minnesota 55410
(612) 929-2800
www.tea2architects.com

Principal Architect: Dan Nepp
Builder: Gary Aulik & Associates
Interior Designer: Bruce Kading of William Beson Interior Design

Page(s): 20, 22 (top left, top middle), 77 (top left), 86 –89, 137 (top right), 161 (top left), 222 (top right, bottom right)

TURNBULL GRIFFIN HAESLOOP
817 Bancroft Way
Berkeley, California 94702
(510) 841-9000
www.tgharchs.com

Principal Architect(s): William Turnbull Jr., Mary Griffin
Builder(s): William Turnbull, Jr., Matthew Sylvia

Page(s): 93 (middle, bottom middle), 142, 196 (top left), 222 (top left), 238 (top right)

Principal Architect(s): William Turnbull Jr., Mary Griffin
Builder(s): Matthew Sylvia

Page(s): 6 (top left), 28, 32–35, 85 (top middle, top right), 152 (top middle), 190 (bottom right), 197 (top right, bottom right)

LANE WILLIAMS ARCHITECTS
327 Second Avenue, West
Seattle, Washington 98119
(206) 284-8355
www.lanewilliams.com

Principal Architect(s): Lane Williams AIA with Michael Auf der Heide
Interior Designer: Pamela Pearce Design, LLC

Page(s): 151, 154–157, 160 (top right, bottom right), 166, 168 (top right), 189 (top right), 206 (top left, bottom left)

design applications, 76–77
effects of, 75
featured home, 78–81
Library walls, 119, 123, 183–85
Light, 8–9, 127–75. *See also* Windows
attraction of, 8–9, 127–33, 140–41
contrast/illusion and, 13
coves, 146, 148
in dark places, 137
defining form, 136
design applications, 128–29,
136–37, 144–46
featured homes, 130–33, 138–41,
147–49
at hallway end, 12, 128
hidden sources, 145
intensity variation, 135–41
on pictures, 129
reflecting surfaces, 9, 140–41,
143–49
shade and, layers of, 136
shelves, 59
stairway lighting, 129
transcendent quality of, 8–9
at tunnel end, 128
to walk toward, 127–33, 140–41
Light fixtures, 47, 143, 146, 148–49
Lipstick, 162, 217
Living rooms (areas)
as alcoves, 43
ceiling height variety, 12–13,
48–51
central, connected, 40–42
changing levels in, 78–80
floating shelves, 49–50, 148–49
as focal gathering place, 84, 86–87
interior views, 56–59
visual weight example, 163–65
Long thin houses, 238, 241–45
Long views through, 54, 56–58,
130–31
Lowered rooms, 76, 78–80

M

Main axis view, 189, 191–93
The march, 196
Mirrors, 146
Movable window walls, 93

N

Nooks, crannies, 39, 40

O

Octagons, 14
Openability, 91–97
containment vs., 100
design applications, 91, 92–93
featured home, 94–97
Openings, in series, 62
Openness. *See also* Expressed
structure
ceiling height variations, 48–51
featured home, 65–67
interior views, 56–59
privacy and, 83–89
reflecting surfaces and, 147–49

sequence of places with, 40–43
Order principles, 9, 14. *See also*
specific principles
Organizing strategy, 237–45
choosing strategy, 244
design applications, 238–40
featured home, 241–45
Outdoor focus, 71
Outdoor rooms, 71. *See also*
Courtyards
Over under, 77

P

Pantheon, 141
Partially hidden rooms, 101
Partially hidden views, 55, 58
Path and place, 22
Patterns/geometries, 179–85
design applications, 180–81
effects of, 179
featured home, 182–85
Pictures, lighted, 129
Place, of quiet remove, 85, 89
Place, of your own, 85, 89
Platforms, 77
Pod of space, 110
Principles of design. *See also specific*
principles
architect toolbox, 7–9
categories, 8–9
fundamental, 6–9
home quality from, 6–7
integrated examples, 14–17
Privacy. *See* Public to private
Proportion, 14, 115
Public to private, 83–89
balanced approach, 83
featured home, 86–89
patterns delineating, 182–85

Q

Quiet places, 85

R

Rafters, exposed, 222
Raised rooms, 77
Receiving place, 22
Reflecting surfaces, 9, 143–49
design applications, 144–46
effects of, 143
featured home, 147–49
varying light intensity, 140–41
Refrains, 197
Repeated themes, 204, 206
Rhythms, 53, 195–201
design applications, 196–97
effects of, 195
featured home, 198–201
rhythms within, 200
Robson Square, 81
Rug-defined place, 31

S

Screen porches, 71, 89
Segmentation, 8, 13, 211. *See also*
Differentiation, of parts; Layering

Sequence of places, 37–43
design applications, 38–39
distinct room perspective vs., 37
featured home, 40–43
modern living and, 37
Shapes
differentiating parts, 110
octagons, 14
windows, 156, 157
Shelter around activity, 29–35
advantages, 29
design applications, 30–31
featured home, 32–34
Shoji screens, 91, 92, 95–97, 100, 179
Signature form, 204
Signature pattern, 205
Simple square/rectangle, 238
Sliding
doors, 67, 73, 91, 92
partitions (panels), 64, 66, 67, 92
screens, 91, 92, 95–97, 100
Soffits, 31, 46
Something places, 231
Southwest light, 138–41
Space. *See also specific elements,*
principles
appearing larger, 43, 61
appearing smaller, 115, 130–31
defined, 8
entryways. *See* Entryways
illusion with, 13
interconnections between, 8
pod of, 110
principles of, 8
segments multiplying, 8, 13
sequence of places, 37–43
shelter around activity, 29–35
Stairways
implied walls around, 114–15
lighting, 129, 130–33
as sculpture, 76, 80
Strategy. *See* Organizing strategy
Surfaces. *See also* Walls
composition, 214, 215–19
continuous, 70
differentiation of parts, 107–10,
111–15
floating, 109
interruption of order, 214
Surprise views, 55
Symmetric alignment, 9, 188, 190,
191–93

T

Texture
design applications, 160–62
differentiating parts, 110
effects of, 159
visual weight, 159–65
on walls/ceilings, 161
Theme/variations, 9, 203–209
design applications, 204–206
effects of, 203
featured home, 207–209

Transitions (outside to in), 27
The triad, 196
TV rooms, 84, 85, 230

V

Vestibules (foyers), 22, 25–27
Views. *See* Inside outside; Interior
views; Windows
Visual weight, 159–65
design applications, 160–62
featured home, 163–65

W

Walls
beltlines, 108, 109, 162
as focal points, 230
headbands, 109, 113–14, 162
implied, 64, 67, 101, 115
insets, 119, 123
library, 119, 123, 183–85
movable window walls, 93
opening up, 65–67
as sculpture, 117, 120, 121–23
sliding partitions, 64, 66, 67, 92
sliding screens, 91, 92, 95–97, 100
textured, 161
thickness, 65–67, 111, 117–23
Wall washing, 9, 144
The waltz, 197
Windows, 87
almost frameless, 70
art glass, 27, 67, 167, 169, 170–75
at axis end, 129
clerestory, 86, 109, 145, 153
corner, 153
daylight fixtures, 152
deep-set, 118, 122–23, 137
in doors, 27
drawing you in, 12
entryways, 25–26, 27
featured homes, 154–57, 170–75
light intensity variation, 135–41
light to walk toward, 8–9, 127–33
movable walls, 93
positioning, 143, 144–45, 151–57,
212, 216, 218–19
privacy and, 168
reflecting surfaces and, 9, 140–41,
143–49
skylights, 80, 81, 140, 143, 153,
225
small panes, 169
translucency ranges, 167–69,
170–75
view, non-view, 167–69, 170–75
wall washing, 9, 144
whimsical use, 153
Window seats, 30, 34, 154–55
Windowsills
height of, 152, 154–56
wide, 119, 123
Wright, Frank Lloyd, 35, 173, 179,
237